Damien has the mos  His
drive, passion, and atte ɔt a
surprise to see him ₁ his
recovery to 0. .

- Che'Vonne Barksdale,B.S., Fitness Center Manager , *Marine Corps Mountain Warfare Training Center*

"Damien has a tremendous work ethic and outstanding researching abilities. He's truly made himself a practitioner of good health and an excellent spokesperson for wellness. Not many people can take their life experiences and convey them to others in a manner that's meaningful. By documenting not only where he's traveled and played, but also taking meticulous notes on health practices and the eating and fitness habits of other countries and cultures, he serves as an excellent contact for those looking for greater insight on health and fitness."

- John Iwanski, *Director of Member and Public Outreach for the American Association of Neurological Surgeons (AANS)*

"As in the teachings of Holistic Health, Damien McSwine entertains and educates us in the underlying cause and origin we fail to consider in today's growing health problems. With a humble appreciation and valid concern for the well being of his fellow man, his insightful journeys around our world, will inspire you to commence one of your own."

- Anonymous Student, *Global College of Natural Medicine*

"The Ancient 20 bridges a perfect gap between cultivation and diversion. I have never had more enjoyment learning about health than with this book. I now have a profound understanding and respect for many other cultures when it comes to life longevity."

- Delisha Milton-Jones, *2-Time Olympic Gold Medalist*

"As a 15 year veteran in the NBA, I certainly understand the importance of sound health principles as the pillars to great health. This is a book that is a must read for my children as well as the elders of my family."

- Theo Ratliff, *Vice-President of the NBA Player's Association* and member of the *Los Angeles Lakers*

"Damien is a very skilled, hard working and dedicated individual with a flare for adding a winning mentality to every situation he is a part of. He is simply helping people that are healthy, sick and shut in live happier, healthier and more optimistic lives.

- Brian Maxwell, best-selling author of *How to Overcome Fear and Create Fortune* founder of NewThoughtGeneration.com

"To be quite honest I have never seen a book with such a theme in any genre. McSwine is creating quite a buzz with his uncanny but yet incredibly simple and antiquated approach to health. I would have never believed that learning to achieve good health could be so simple."

- Koko Ishe, author of *The 7 Great Lies All Christians Tell*

"Modernization and globalization has not only narrowed the physical demarcation of geographical borders, but it has also promoted many unhealthy practices that contribute to the increasing statistics of all types of lifestyle diseases. Damien makes it palpably clear that healthy eating and healthy living are two of the most important pillars on which a healthy lifestyle rest. His humanitarianism is capsulated in this unselfish and reservedly profound masterpiece that will help the reader to appreciate the simple and most viable approach to living a long and healthy life."

- Noreen Greenwood, *Office of Deputy Principal at University of the West Indies-Mona in Kingston, Jamaica*

"This is an idea whose time has come. The Ancient 20 reaches across the oceans and brings valuable cultural and personally experienced information that can aid and be healthful to our present world health care crisis."

- Phillip J. Oliver, AAS, *Sickle Cell Foundation*

THE
ANCIENT
20:
TWENTY ANCIENT HEALTH LAWS REVEALED FROM TWENTY COUNTRIES

Discovering a new approach to health through adventure and simplicity

DAMIEN MCSWINE
FOREWORD BY DR. JOEL WALLACH

By DAMIEN MCSWINE

© 2011 P.I. Health Group LLC. All rights reserved.

First Edition, 2011
1 3 5 7 9 10 8 6 4 2

Visit our Web site at **www.privateeyehealth.com**

No Part of this publication may be reproduced, stored in a retrieval system, or transmitted in any form or by any means—electronic, mechanical, photocopy, recording, or any other—except for brief quotations in printed reviews, without the prior permission of the author.

Disclaimer: The Publisher and the Author make no representations or warranties with respect to the accuracy or completeness of the contents of this work and specifically disclaim all warranties, including without limitation warranties of fitness for a particular purpose. No warranty may be created or suitable for every situation. This work is sold with the understanding that the publisher is not engaged in rendering legal, accounting, or other professional services. If professional assistance is required, the services of a competent professional person should be sought. Neither the Publisher nor the Author(s) shall be liable for damages arising herefrom. The fact that an organization or website is referred to in this work as a citation and/or a potential source of further information does not mean that the Author or Publisher endorses the information the organization or website may provide or recommendations it may make. Further, readers should be aware that internet websites listed in this work may have changed or disappeared between when this work was written and when it is read.

Printed in the United States of America

Library of Congress Registration Number: TXU001736590

ISBN: 9781466423589

Designed by Grafix Valley

Visit us at **www.privateeyehealth.com** for free information, videos and online content.

ACKNOWLEDGEMENTS

This book is dedicated God. Without you, nothing is possible! Thank you for using me as a conduit to distribute insightful information that may bring value to the lives of others. And to my parents Myron and Lela who have shaped me to be the best that I can be. They have been with me through the highs and lows of life and have always instilled in me to be the best that I could be in life. Nothing is possible without you! Thank you.

It is impossible for me to name the innumerable people who have influenced my life and this book. I must, give thanks to the people who have been instrumental throughout this writing: Marcel Turner, Mylika Johnson and Barbara Lukehart.

A special thank you goes Dr. Joel Wallach, author of the world famous book "Dead Doctors Don't Lie." It is through Wallach's life changing naturopathic research that numerous lives have been saved. His ground breaking knowledge on health and illness has given tens of thousands a renewed sense of empowerment. Dr. J as many affectionately call him, has dedicated more than 50 years of service to helping mankind find answers to its health issues. It has been under Wallach's tutelage that I have truly been able to learn, apply and comprehend the role that nutrition plays in disease and healing. Thanks Doc!

In closing I wish to acknowledge those who are no longer with us and who have invested so much into my life. Easter McSwine, Welton McSwine II, Robert McSwine, Cedric McSwine, Travis Teague, Khris Rushing, Lois Gordon, Inieke Udoiwod, Fred Owens, Phil Oliver, Magnolia Ford, Colin Marshall, Marc Fulcher, Eloise Turner-Mitchell, Joseph Cassey and many more. Thanks so much for leaving an impression on my life. This book is in honor of you as many of you left this earth without proper information concerning health.

CONTENTS

FOREWORD

Damien McSwine, a young American athlete, has sustained a form of "shuttle diplomacy," as he has traveled the world in pursuit of athletic excellence. With the practiced eye of a professional athlete, he has observed and recorded cultural practices that contribute to health and longevity around the world.

From dietary practices, exercise and sleep habits, Damien has recorded universal cultural "secrets" that can be easily explored by each and every one of us, without great expense or without the need for expensive facilities or equipment. Unfortunately, America has sought the advice of "high tech" written medical advice on how to live a long healthful life. In 1990, Americans ranked 17th in longevity. In 2000, Americans ranked 24th. In 2005, Americans ranked 46th and in 2009 Americans came in at a staggering 50th in longevity. Obviously the route we have chosen to follow was a poor choice.

Humans require 90 essential nutrients to optimize their health and longevity. When we disregard this formula, we pay the price. A simple life with modest exercise, a calorie restricted diet and high nutrient density per calorie (obtained through quality food and supplementation) are the secrets to a long, productive and quality life.

Thank you, Damien, for compiling the world's healthful practices under simple cover and analyzing them for us, with the eyes of a professional athlete.

Dr. Joel D. Wallach, BS, DVM, ND

INTRODUCTION

In an ever-changing country, with medical coverage at an all time high, citizens of the United States have not received the medical education that equates to a high quality of overall health. People will spend their last dime in an effort to get medical knowledge. That same knowledge may have put them in their diseased state in the first place.

As new health legislation bills are being passed, the future of the U.S. health care system does not appear to be very appealing for anyone. If we think back to the times of our ancestors, we will find that they lived longer lives with fewer resources than we have today. How they prepared the food, the methods for fertilization, and the drinks they consumed, all played a part in their long life spans.

My sincerest hope is that this book will give to you everything that it has given to me in allowing me to become a healthier individual. I am now more cognoscente of simple treatments for small ailments that have been known to produce big results. As a professional basketball player, I have traveled to over 35 countries and lived in at least 20 of them. It was a great honor for me to have the opportunity to learn amongst other cultures and witness their eating habits, sleeping patterns, cornerstone foods, etc. While traveling throughout Europe, South America, Caribbean, Middle East, and Asia I frequently saw people living to be 100 years old and upward. I knew that as a country we had more resources than they did so, there was a method to their magic and I wanted to find out what it was that they did. Until this year, I had never met anyone who lived in the United States who was more than 95 years of age.

The oldest living relative of mine that lives in the United States is 80 years of age. With all of the modern technology that we have in America it was evident to me that we had gotten away from the "simple things in life", which are proper diet and the ingestion of minerals and vitamins, as well as other essential nutrients. We are now so advanced that we have outsmarted ourselves. My journeys have shown me that simplicity is still very effective and still exists in many countries today.

The following information is the true story of my journey and many of the values which I have encountered along the way. You may find many different benefits from this book, which help improve your quality of life. Each chapter contains a personal story from a different country in which I have lived during the course of my world travels. Again this information is not intended to replace medical advice.

Damien McSwine

GOD'S MESSAGE ABOUT DIET

Genesis 6:3.

"And the Lord said, My spirit shall not always strive with man, for that he also is flesh: yet his days shall be an hundred and twenty years."

Genesis 1:29

"Then God said, "I give you every seed-bearing plant on the face of the whole earth and every tree that has fruit with seed in it. They will be yours for food."

Deuteronomy 8:8

A land of wheat, and barley, and vines, and fig trees, and pomegranates; a land of olive oil, and honey.

Genesis 43:11

Then their father Israel said to them, "If it must be, then do this: Put some of the best products of the land in your bags and take them down to the man as a gift--a little balm and a little honey, some spices and myrrh, some pistachio nuts and almonds.

Ezekiel 47:12

Fruit trees of all kinds will grow on both banks of the river. Their leaves will not wither, nor will their fruit fail. Every month they will bear, because the water from the sanctuary flows to them. Their fruit will serve for food and their leaves for healing."

HOW IT ALL BEGAN

With 13 seconds remaining on the clock, the stadium was loud but quiet. You could feel the tension like a sharp knife blade. I saw the faces of fans so unsure about the future of their lives based on the next 13 seconds. Mothers and fathers were thinking about what they would tell their kids, gamblers were waiting to cash in, everyone was nervous... I knew it, because so was I. As my teammates and I came out of that huddle, I went blank. I honestly could not tell you what I was thinking during those last 13 seconds or even what I did. All I know is that when the buzzer sounded more than two thousand screaming fans rushed the court screaming and hugging me, "ganamos, ganamos, somos campeones!" It was like an explosion of happiness, the noise was like the sound of a raging sea mixed with fireworks on the fourth of July. Tears of joy, disbelief and relief filled the Fabio Gonzalez Basketball Arena in Puerto Plata, Dominican Republic.

All I did was hit a shot; but to the people I did more than that. We had broken a twenty year curse of not winning a championship for the team known as Las Cotorras Del Gustavo. I'd seen concerts of fans crying when they watched Michael Jackson perform; but I was now seeing people cry at a winning basketball game. I had made the game winning shot and gave our team the title. They chanted MVP as I was awarded the Most Valuable Player; I reflected as I hoisted up the trophy and thought my career was finally going in the direction I dreamed about as a child and collegiate athlete.

After experiencing such a high I decided to stay in Puerto Plata and celebrate with the team for about two weeks. I needed the rest and the season had drained me physically and mentally.

Closer to the end of the season I had been experiencing some pain in my foot that was hindering me from practicing or walking without a limp so I decided to consult a few of our team officials. After speaking with team management, I went to have my foot looked at by a local orthopedic doctor. Upon consulting with the doctor he informed me that I would need surgery right away, to remove a bunion that had formed on my toe. Doctor Cabrera explained that this was an issue that began long before I was an adult because of my flat feet. Ten years prior to this point my parents had been very adamant about me getting the surgery on my foot before the condition progressed. My answer to them was that I could not afford to sit down for 3 months, but I guess when you're young your parents don't know anything. I could hear their voices in the back of my mind as the doctor broke the news to me.

Feeling dejected after hearing the news, my mind began to move at one hundred miles-an-hour. The thought that this surgery could possibly keep me down for six months or more before full recovery was quite scary. I counseled with several people before the surgery with regards to where I should have it done. I had insurance outside of the United States but not inside.

The out-of-pocket costs of a surgery of this magnitude could run between $10,000 and $15,000.

Although my team and insurance would be covering the expenses of the surgery in the DR, many of my family members who live in the Dominican Republic scoffed at the idea that I would even consider doing a surgery in their country, when it was clear that their medical system was not as good as the one in the United States.

Against everyone's advice I decided to have the surgery done in the DR. Stupido, idiota, ignorante, loco and barbaro were just a few of the names that were thrown at me for my decision. The phrase, "All free things wind up being expensive in the end", had never meant so much to me prior to the day of my surgery. As of November 26, 2008, my life had changed forever. I was told that I would be ready to return to the court by March of 2009 but that did not happen. Complication after complication became my norm following the foot surgery.

To make matters worse, I was in a foreign land away from my comfort zone. I had two nails sticking out of my foot and an ace bandage wrap. Right away I figured something weird was going on because my foot was not put in a cast. In the DR things are not as developed as I was accustomed to so my recovery was a bit tougher. Every day I had to send someone to a drug store to buy injections and medications for me.

Not only did they have to buy the injections but they also had to find a local nurse in the neighborhood to come and give me the injections on a daily basis. What a circus! The New Year had passed and we were approaching the 10th day of January in 2009. I was not in the greatest of spirits because I could sense that the two year relationship with the woman that I was dating was soon coming to an end. One day, I received a teammate who stopped by to visit and check on me. He kept staring at my foot in deep concern and asking several questions. I could feel his eyes dissecting my foot as if he was a surgeon and for some reason I felt his concern the more he looked at my foot.

We made small talk about how things were going with his family and he jumped on his moped and proceeded to leave.

His last words before he left was, "Tienes que ir al medico de una vez, porque se parece que tienes una infeccion."

The translation was that I needed to go see a doctor right away because it looked like I had an infection. I didn't want to believe him but he spoke with such conviction and assurance that I could not ignore what he said. Two minutes later I was on the back of a scooter on my way to see Doctor Cabrera!

The doctor had informed me that I did have an infection and that he would have to go back in and operate to clean out the infection.

Over the course of this chapter I will use the analogy of a car to convey to you my physical and mental states of being during specific points throughout my recovery. So at this point, I would like for you to imagine a car completely out of gas. Not only is that car out of gas but now it is out of oil because someone has drained the oil from it. That car was me. I was totally out of it mentally after hearing that I had an infection. The thought of having more surgery only meant that I would have to remain away from the game of basketball for a longer period of time. It was a quick outpatient surgery and four days later I was back to the norm. I was instructed to go to the emergency if after three days my foot was still swollen. Low and behold my foot continued to swell and I had to return two days later.

This time Doctor Cabrera was not there but his colleague Dr. Lopez was the doctor on staff at the time. Dr. Lopez was very familiar with me because of my visits with his partner. After surveying my foot and looking at my bandages he regretfully informed me that the infection was still present and that he was going to try and cure it manually. He also did not hesitate in letting me know that there was a chance that my foot could be amputated, depending on how bad the infection was. What? My foot cut off? Am I in a nightmare?

This is not supposed to happen to me.

Curing the infection manually meant that he was going to have to go in and scrape away the infection with tools and push out the infection by applying pressure on the outside of the skin. There was no anesthesia or painkillers administered. This seemed to be a medical procedure from the 1500's or something out of a movie. I was desperate to get rid of the infection so I agreed. The process was some of the most pain that I have ever felt. Imagine the car again with no gas and no oil. Now, two tires have been removed from the car. This was me. The doctors "manually cured" the infection four times over the course of a week before they declared my foot healed. I was very stoic in my reaction to the "good news."

Based on my small knowledge of infections I knew that there was no way that I could go from having the threat of getting my foot cut off to being healed in four days by the hands of two, third- world country doctors. I am an optimist but the probability of that happening was next to zero. A few days had gone by and I had been out of contact from the rest of the world so I decided to check my Skype voicemail through my computer. Upon opening my messages I noticed that I had three messages from the same number which was my brother Duerod in Chicago. Duerod is not my blood brother but we share a bond as if we were. The first message I heard said, "Damien, our brother Gill is in the hospital because he wasn't feeling good so he checked himself in." Duerod's second message was quite encouraging but still somewhat concerning. It said, "They are running some tests on Gill because he not responding to the medications and he's experiencing some complications with his liver. We are going to pray he comes out ok." My level of concern rose after the second message but it had not reached panic. Due's third message dropped me to my knees. "Damien our brother Gill is gone man, he passed this morning. You have to come home." Due did his best to deliver the message in a strong fashion but even he crumbled towards the end before he hung up. How does a healthy 26 year old drive himself to the hospital, get admitted and never come out? Remember the car analogy? Now imagine the car with no gas, no oil, no tires and parts missing from the car. The car cannot be driven at all. This car was me.

I arrived in Chicago late night on March 5th for Gill's funeral the next day. Limping and completely out of energy I managed to get through an extremely difficult day. I was not sure where my life was headed and why all of these things were happening to me but the only thing that I had was my faith to keep me going.

To say that I felt low would not do my emotional state any justice. That night while eating with family and friends, I was to receive another revelation. A family friend named Commie, who worked in the medical industry as a pharmacist for years, noticed the inflammation and discoloration of my foot. Without hesitation, in her strong Nigerian accent, she said, "Boy, You'd better go get your foot looked at by a doctor right now, because it looks like you have an infection. I know an infection when I see one and I'm quite sure you have one. You need to go tonight if you can!" I registered what she said but because of my state of mind I was no longer concerned about my foot anymore. I just wanted peace of mind.

Gill was a very encouraging voice throughout my career and he always reminded me that I could do better on and off the court. Life without him would be an adjustment for certain. After winding down for a few days and soaking in the fact that Gill would no longer be around, I decided that I was going to take heed to Commie's advice and go see a doctor. I had not yet been to my home in Detroit prior to arriving in Chicago, so I boarded a train and scheduled an appointment to see my local foot doctor there.

As my luck would have it, my local podiatrist Dr. Lee was on vacation and would not be back for two weeks.

I opted to see one of his partners named Dr. Kissel.

The fact that I was seeing a doctor in the United States provided me with a level of comfort that I had not felt in over seven months.

During the visit with Dr.Kissel, I explained my situation and the course of events over the past six to seven months. The first thing he did was take X-rays of my foot to assess the damage that was done. He looked at the X-rays and he looked back at me with the look of a person that had seen a ghost, and removed his glasses from his face.

In a very disappointed but concerned tone he said, "Who did your surgery? And was he wearing a wig when he did it? I have never witnessed such a botched foot surgery in my twenty years of practicing medicine. The doctor in the Dominican completely destroyed your cartilage and bone in your foot. He fixed your foot as if you were a 75 year old who will not walk again. Not to mention, it appears as though you still have an infection that they claimed to have cleaned up. Let's hope the infection has not gotten in the bone because that could mean an amputation. As far as you playing again I don't know how that could happen because so much damage is done. I'm going to give Dr. Lee a call and let him know what's going on with you. It's going to take an extensive amount of work just to get you to the point of walking normal again."

I was somewhat hurt by the information but I held out hope because I had the confidence in Dr. Lee's abilities to get me back to my normal self. When Dr. Lee returned I went in for a visit. By this time he had already been privy to my case from his partner Dr. Kissel. While putting his hand on my back as a father would do a son, Dr. Lee said, "Damien, it's time for you to think about a career change. You won't be able to play basketball anymore not even recreationally.

What we need to concentrate on is figuring out how we can re-construct the bone in your foot and toe. I'm not quite sure what can be done at this point but I'm certain that you won't be able to play anymore. I'm sorry Damien, I know how dedicated to the game of basketball you are."

Let's re-visit the car analogy. There is now a car with no gas, no oil, no tires, and missing parts. Now the engine and transmission have been removed. The car is now ready for the junk yard and can officially be scraped for metal.

After Dr. Lee informed me that I would not be able to play again, I had hit the lowest point of my life.

Two more doctors eventually confirmed what Dr. Kissel and Dr. Lee had informed me. There was to be no more basketball. Rock bottom seemed like the ideal vacation compared to where I was, but something told me to continue searching for a solution.

The most urgent issue that needed to be resolved was that of the infection in my foot. I quickly got insurance and went to see the head doctor of Orthopedics at a local hospital in Detroit. Doctor V was practically a genius in medicine. He performed two surgeries on my foot in two days and it was confirmed three months later that the infection was gone. The infection was gone but the fact still remained that I walked with a limp and I needed to repair the cartilage and bone in my foot. Every doctor I went to after wanted to fuse my toe which would guarantee that I had zero chance of returning to do anything which required bending my toe. It is important to remember that this was my big toe which functions as the body's primary source of balance and spring from the ground.

I continued researching doctors around the country that did advanced procedures to repair feet or toes.

I ran across Dr. Richard who was the only individual who actually believed that he could perform a surgery that may work out for me. He was located in Orlando, Florida. Of course he could provide no guarantees but he provided hope, and a chance, which was all I wanted. I could not in good conscious allow a doctor to operate on me if he did not believe that I could get better, so I purposely dismissed any doctor who was unsure of their methods or outcomes. Needless to say Dr. Richard did the surgery and after three days I was back home in Detroit recovering. The surgery was quite complex as Dr. Richard had to place a piece of titanium in my toe, graft bone into my metatarsal and place plastic in the top portion of the toe.

It was a total toe joint replacement surgery. These kinds of surgeries almost never happen to anyone under the age of 50 or 60. By the numbers, no athlete (professional or amateur) has ever gotten a total toe replacement surgery done and continued to play. It has just never happened. Dr. Richard reminded me that everything would be up to me if I were to ever return to play. I was not concerned with history or with those that had come before me.

It was too difficult and expensive to take trips back and forth to Orlando, so I made an agreement to consult with Dr. V at the local hospital, while going through the recovery process.

The irony of this situation is that Dr. V was one of the doctors who wanted to fuse my toe and told me that toe replacement was not an option because there had already been a serious infection in the bone. In fact all doctors reminded me that I would be risking life and limb by putting metal where there was an infection prior. Dr. V treated me but throughout the entire time he felt that the toe replacement would not work. I could sense, that he almost wanted to be right and have the toe joint fail. I on the other hand, wanted to make history in returning to the game of basketball.

It dawned on me that I could possibly be treading on land that no one had ever touched before, metaphorically speaking. I was nervous (of the unknown) but yet excited at the same time.

Realizing that I had a tough battle on my hands I decided to seek out one of the best Naturopathic Doctors in the world. Dr. Joel Wallach explained to me that I needed to be diligent in taking nutrients and changing certain small habits of my life if I wanted to get better. I began my recovery by prayer and visualization, taking a host of nutritional supplements and most importantly applying many of the Ancient 20 Health Laws that I learned while traveling the world. These simple principles have played such a big role in my return to the court that I felt compelled to share them with the world.

I am currently entering my second season after my recovery. I am so thankful and so grateful for the opportunity to share my adventures with you. I know that I am merely a minuscule member in the industry of healthcare. I am not a doctor, I am not a nurse nor do I have health-related degree or certificate in medicine. What I do have is the desire to be healthy in life as we all do.

This book is my best attempt to share the little that I know.

Law One

WATER CONSUMPTION IS THE INFRASTRUCTURE TO GREAT HEALTH: "VENEZUELA"

"We forget that the water cycle and the life cycle are one."
~Jacques Cousteau

While I was vacationing in the Caribbean, I received a phone call from my agent asking me if I was physically fit and ready to play. I was still unwinding from a grueling season in Macedonia, so I told him that I needed a few more days of rest, but that I would be ready, as long as the money was right. When he mentioned Venezuela, I knew that the money would be right. We negotiated the terms and within 48 hours I was signed to play for the "Marinos de Anzoategui".

This team, which was stationed in Puerto La Cruz, won championships many times over the last decade. Just mention Puerto La Cruz to anyone living in Venezuela and they will tell you that Puerto La Cruz is one of the most beautiful places in the entire country. It's notorious for its landscape, as the city has a beautiful beach that attracts tourists from around the world. The cost of living is high but that didn't matter since I didn't have to pay for anything. The team was owned by a wealthy gentleman who also owned television and radio networks and a professional soccer team. Needless to say, our team had the best of everything! As a basketball player who strives to play at the highest level possible, I had participated in a NBA training camp (Chicago Bulls 2003), which ended in my release from the team.

The purpose of mentioning the NBA is to say that if there was ever a feeling of playing "professional" basketball outside of the United States, it was the feeling I had while playing in Venezuela. Every game was televised; people stopped me in the street to take my picture or asked for my autograph and every "away game" required airline travel. This experience was truly first class in its entirety. To top it all, each player was assigned a "personal driver," who picked us up whenever we wished and took us shopping, out to eat, or anywhere else we desired to venture.

My time in Venezuela was among the most fun I had ever experienced, while playing professional basketball. The downside to playing there, however, was the "scorching heat." Our coach was Brazilian, and he loved working us hard. So, for practice I had better be well rested and ready to "perform" every single day. The native players loved to play fast paced ball and were very physical. Punches to the midsection, elbows, and scratched eyes were just some of the entrees served up during practice. I didn't mind this aspect of the game; in fact, it took me back to how I was raised playing the game in Detroit, Michigan. But one thing that Detroit did not prepare me for was the "constant dehydration" that I experienced in Venezuela. I believe in doing everything to the best of my ability, so I never missed practice and my intensity was constant during games.

As a result of playing so hard, I left three games with bad leg cramps and full body cramps, which left me incapacitated for a day or two. Luckily, I never had a game the following day when that occurred.

The pain that one goes through, during dehydration, is a process that can reduce the strongest person to a helpless newborn baby. The body becomes weak and depleted and in order to regain strength, has to be rehydrated intravenously. Anyone who has experienced dehydration is well aware of the pain that comes with it!

If I wanted to continue to play my best in Venezuela, I realized that some adjustments had to be made. On game day I loved to be the first player in the gym and get a good warm up before game time. For the very first time in my basketball career, my work ethics had worked against me. Due to the climate in South America, my body needed something more because I was sweating profusely and losing plenty of minerals, as well as water. Sweat is a soup of vital nutrients (primarily water) that your body expels during exercise or other forms of activity. The more you sweat and fail to replenish those nutrients the faster your body becomes closer to breaking down or becoming ill.

After my third incident with dehydration my Venezuelan teammates started giving me cups of water (although I later came to find out that I was mineral deficient) before the start of the game. The gymnasiums where the games are played have no air conditioning and many times I would sweat a lot before the games began. My teammates would say things like "tienes que beber agua!" which means "you have to drink water." This was very a nostalgic experience because it reminded me of my brother back home in Detroit.

Marcel, my younger brother, was in the habit of filling up big jugs of water and keeping one with him wherever he went. He would do this every day and I just took it as being a weird habit. He made sure he drank at least a gallon of water every day. By the time he came home from work his jug of water was empty.

The part that I find extremely ironic - as I am writing in this very moment - is that my brother is 27 years old and I have never known him to have any illnesses other than a common cold. While I, prior to my knowledge of the importance of water consumption would get minor illnesses very easy. Marcel's daily consumption of water has largely contributed to his good health.

Dr. Jennifer Daniels, of Harvard University, informs us that dehydration is one of the top for leading causes of death in the world. Dr. Daniels paints a great example of how dehydration affects the body. In her famed lecture titled, *Slave Quarter Cures*, Daniels states, "Imagine a road in front of a major building blocked off without detour signs. Then, block off the next road. Then block off another. It wouldn't be long until no one could get to this building and the building could not function. Picture that building as your kidney, heart or lungs. That is what dehydration does." Daniels continues by saying, "The only thing that gets stuff where it has to go in your body is the water waves, through the blood system by circulation. When dehydration occurs, your immune system makes a decision on which organs will go without nutrition. As a result the blood has less and less water, and it gets tougher and tougher to pump, because of its' thickness. This is how heart attacks happen in the middle of the night. So, the best thing to do is to have a glass of water before you go to bed."

I had to find out the hard way but shortly thereafter I made water one of my biggest allies.

It is noteworthy that the human body is made up of approximately three-fourths (75%) water. Needless to say, water plays a huge part in our survival.

Ancient 20's Teaching Points on WATER:

- Water is 83% of Blood

    75% of Muscle

    74% of the Brain

    22% of Bone

    20% of Fat

85% of Heart

80% of Lungs

- Helps prevent kidney stones, as well as constipation

- Being lean is much better because muscle holds more water than fat

- Your lungs will lose about 3 cups of water daily just from normal breathing

- Water reduces hunger. That is why you can survive for much longer with water than with food. (This is extremely relevant because there have been many studies done on people thinking they are hungry, when they are truly thirsty)

- 12 trips to the bathroom dispel roughly 6 cups of water

- Promotes blood circulation

- Hydrates the skin and removes toxins.

Particularly relevant is when God created the earth he covered it in two-thirds (66%) of water! The purpose of drinking water is to hydrate and flush the system. To make sure you are drinking the adequate amount of water, you can take your weight (let's say, for example – you weigh 160 pounds) and divide it in half (80 pounds) and change the "pounds" to "ounces" (therefore 80 ounces instead of 80 pounds), and then you'll be drinking half of your body size in water (mathematically speaking).

For diabetics, the best thing for you to do is drink one glass of water with meals and between meals. It's also better to take water breaks instead of coffee breaks. If you are looking to overcome any physical condition as diabetes, your water intake is essential to becoming healthier. Water carries important things like nutrients throughout the body to the places that need to have them but also is responsible for removing the bad things from the body.

Climate will naturally play a significant part in how much water you should drink. I would not drink the same amount of water in Venezuela as I would if I were in Russia or Antarctica. South America's climate conditions call for more water consumption than that of other continents. So, consider your weight, health conditions and your climate to determine the amount of water you should drink. Most importantly, make sure that you drink water every day, as it is the building block to enhance your health.

Law Two

YOUR BED IS YOUR BEST FRIEND: "KOSOVO"

"Sleep is the golden chain that ties health and our bodies together." ~Thomas Dekker

Become a lover of rest! It is through resting that the body replenishes. In 2005, I had the opportunity of playing in a country where most people would not dare tread. Kosovo. Prior to my arrival, the country was on the tail end of recovering from a war of independence against Serbia. Americans were well received there because of the assistance that the country acquired from President Bill Clinton during their conflicts with Serbia. African-Americans on the contrary, are rarely seen in Kosovo, so they tend to attract stares everywhere they go. If you happen to be an African-American in Kosovo, then chances are you're working with the United Nations. The UN has a program that pays Americans and other foreigners very well to work as a Corrections Officer in the local penal system.

I was lucky to be stationed in Phristine, which is the capital. I couldn't imagine what life would have been like had I played with a team in one of the more desolate areas of the country. Kosovo is located in the southern part of the former Yugoslavian republic. To say that it was freezing cold there would be the world's biggest understatement. Although we practiced inside a gymnasium most days during practice, all of the players practiced in full body jogging suits. You could actually see the air smoke when you conversed with someone!

As a child, I never liked going to sleep before 10 pm. But my childish desire was never realized, as my father was a military veteran and believed in going to bed early and waking up early. During my time in Kosovo, I played some of my best basketball and our team won the championship that year. I knew that my performance was due to something in my daily regimen, but I could not quite pinpoint which part of the routine. We practiced two times per day, once in the morning and once at night. To help the time move faster, I used to sleep between practices for about 2 hours. After the second practice I would come home, watch a DVD and be in bed by 10:15 almost every night!

During this time period the television series, "24", had just come out for sale on DVD, so I and the other two American players bought the entire series of "24" and "OZ." We could not wait to get home after each practice and watch every hour episode of these shows. These shows became the topics of our conversations on road game trips or at team dinners. Unless you have lived abroad, you can't imagine how the little things make you feel at home when you are in a foreign country. Prior to this time I had never been the guy to be in bed before midnight during my adult years.

By resting, I found that I had fewer injuries and sicknesses. I woke up every morning by 6am on my own volition, and I was always sharp throughout the day. It is through sleep that the body replenishes itself. Sleep is the time your hair, skin, and nails grow. Still don't believe me? Compare the 40 year old who eats a balanced diet, supplemented with mineral and vitamin nutrition, has a head full of hair, and gets good rest each day, as opposed to the 30 year old "party animal" who looks old in the face, lives on coffee, has thinning hair, and who is always sick. In large part, this is due to the fact that the "party animal" doesn't allow their body a chance to rejuvenate itself.

To further expand upon the importance of rest, I will use my grandfather as an example. My grandfather is currently 80 years of age. During his early 40's he was diagnosed with Type II onset diabetes. The majority of individuals whom I know who have diabetes usually have bouts with blood circulation, low energy levels, trouble with wound healing and many other complications (*see Dr. Joel Wallach*). Every since I was born I have never known my grandfather to have ANY illness or complication related to diabetes. This is a very important point because normally as one gets older the body system begins to slow down making life more challenging for any senior citizen that has a health issue. On his job he puts tremendous stress on his body. He has worked for more than 35 years with a cement company called "Mississippi Materials" located in Greenwood, Mississippi. Pouring concrete and lifting heavy metals, cement mixes and tools is not an easy job for anyone let alone an 80 year old man. Every morning he gives himself an injection of insulin, watches his favorite cartoon (Scooby Doo), while making his breakfast, and goes about his day as anyone else would. The secret to his "seamless health" can be linked to his sleeping patterns. He is in bed by nine o'clock pm every night! It does not matter even if he has a visitor from the other side of the world; he NEVER deviates from his scheduled hours of rest. I now fully understand how he has risen from bed every morning by 4:30 am and has left from the house to work by 5:30 am for the last 40 years.

I am quite certain that everyone has been told that they should get rest, but the part that gets untold is why rest is essential. Getting rest may seem insignificant, but while sleeping, your body has a chance to heal and replenish. The more rest, the longer your body has to recharge.

Ancient 20's teaching points on REST:

- Helps the body make repairs – While you are sleeping your, body repairs itself from ultra-violet rays and other harmful exposures. Sleep deprivation alters immune function, including the activity of the body's killer cells, which are a part of our innate immune system and are responsible for killing cells infected with a given virus. Your cells produce more white proteins when you are sleeping.

- May help you lose weight – A research supported by the *American Thoracic Society* shows that those who sleep less than 5 hours a night have a higher chance of being over weight.

- Reduce Stress - When the body lacks rest, it goes into a state of stress. Sleep deprivation causes stress to all of your body's organs because they are working a double shift. This will eventually cause them to breakdown.

- May Prevent Cancer – Those who stay up late, until the early morning hours, are at higher risk for breast cancer and colon cancer. This is believed to be the case because this association is caused by differing levels of melatonin in people who are exposed to light at night. Being exposed to light reduces the levels of melatonin, a hormone in our bodies that regulates the circadian rhythm (human body clock) and is said to protect us against cancer.

- Hair, Skin Cells, and Nails Grow - These 3 are the most visible regenerative cells that we have and it is through sleeping that they grow. The less sleep you get, the more each will be stunted.

- Improves Your Mood - Sleep loss may result in irritability, impatience, inability to concentrate, and moodiness. Too little sleep can also leave you too tired to do the things you enjoy.

- Increases Memory and Learning Capacity - Sleep helps the brain to commit new information to memory. According to a 2005 research done by experts from Boston's *Beth Israel Deaconess Hospital and Matthew Walker PhD,* when you are asleep, "It seems as though you are shifting memory to more efficient storage regions within the brain. Consequently, when you awaken, memory tasks can be performed both more quickly and accurately, and with less stress and anxiety."

• Safety - A lack of sleep contributes to a greater tendency to fall asleep during the daytime. These lapses may cause falls and mistakes such as medical errors, air traffic mishaps, and road accidents.

In conclusion, rest is one of the few things in life that you do not have to pay for. The trick, however, is that if you don't rest now you will pay later; chances are the price will be costly. Your body keeps an internal running tab of everything you do. Working those double-shifts on a constant basis may work while you are twenty-five but you will feel those, "extra working hours", when you are in your fifties. Successful businessmen and women have known this secret for ages. Your most productive hours of the day when your brain is sharp are when you wake early. An unspoken advantage of getting in bed early is that you can get up earlier the next morning and get more accomplished. Instead of 7 am you will be rising at 5 am, which makes your days longer and gives you more time to do daily activities. Most times I'm done with everything I have to do for the day by 11am, because I get to bed as early as 9 pm and rise as early as 4:30 am.

Law Three

SWIMMING IS NOT LIMITED TO FISH: "LEBANON"

"The water is your friend. You don't have to fight with water, just share the same spirit as the water and it will help you move." ~Aleksandr Popov

In 2003, I had the opportunity to go to the country of Lebanon. In light of the September 11th attacks, it was a tough decision to make. I previously had turned down a contract to go to there in 2001. When the offer was presented to me a second time, I felt that God was giving me a sign to go and check it out. So, I went. While there, I was living in a nice loft off the Mediterranean Sea, in the capital city of *Beirut*.

I couldn't help but to think that I could not be in the same war torn Beirut that had taken the lives of many Americans during the "Beirut Bombings" decades ago. Indeed I was in Beirut! I immediately met a few people with whom I could hang out. One gentleman in particular was about 55 years old and he was the assistant coach of another team in the league in which I was to play. I had met him on the airplane on the way to Beirut when we were both watching a fight on the plane in which the airline pilots were forced to make an emergency landing in Budapest, Hungary and remove the assailants. It was quite a show to see the airline stewardesses trying to breakup a vicious fight. This coach was an Armenian gentleman who worked hard and tough hours to establish himself as one of the best jewelers in Miami, Florida.

He had moved back home to Lebanon to relax. He would routinely come and retrieve me and another Lebanese player named Henne to go out, eat and talk. He came to be known as "Uncle Joe". Uncle Joe was always alive, vibrant and never really tired. Because I was young and hungry for wealth I would always question Uncle Joe on the steps he took to make his fortune as a jeweler. For as impressed as I was about his wealth I was even more galvanized by his energy level for his age. So, one day I asked him his secret to staying in shape. He looked at me and said "Don't worry nephew I will show you tomorrow", promising me that he would share his secret with me the following day after practice.

As promised, he picked me up and took me to the Mediterranean Sea. Before jumping into the water he looked at me as if he was giving me the keys to a Rolls Royce and he said, "This is what I do." He jumped in and started swimming laps! There was a buoy about one-hundred meters away that he liked to swim to. I just so happened to have basketball shorts on so I also jumped in and started swimming laps. I stayed in for a short period compared to Uncle Joe. The key to the "pep in his step" was swimming 3 to 4 times weekly. I immediately started researching what this really did for the body. I was honestly amazed at what it did for him and it opened up another chapter for me to cardiovascular health.

In the United States I had seen many senior citizens swimming on several occasions, but I had paid it no mind because I thought that they just liked to swim. There have been countless times in the past that I have gone to swimming pools and witnessed water aerobics classes taking place. I realized that this was an alternative way for people to stay in shape. The buoyancy of water acts naturally to form a protective cocoon around the body which takes away, excess pressure on the bones or joints.

Two years after my stay in Lebanon, I broke the *calcaneal* bone in my foot. My doctor (Dr. Lee) recommended that I get in the pool for physical therapy. I wasn't able to run or walk so I needed a way to challenge myself to stay in physical shape. As a professional athlete, I have had to endure some of the world's toughest coaches and withstand some of the grittiest conditioning programs never witnessed by most athletes, but swimming was in a class of it's own as far as preparing my body for the rigors of the sport of basketball.

I must tell you that, "a half mile in the swimming pool is not even in the same category as a half mile jogging". The irony of the entire situation is that I could only do one lap in the pool without stopping. There were about three elderly men who would come in every morning while I was doing my therapy and swim for 45 minutes to an hour, WITHOUT STOPPING! After about one month of constant practice I eventually reached the point to where I could swim about 40 laps without stopping. The critical point for my improvement was discovered in my learning to "breathe" the correct way while swimming. Swimming allowed me to burn twice the number of calories I did than when I was jogging or climbing stairs!

Another benefit to swimming is that the body temperature never rises while exercising. This is mainly because you are swimming in water that is fairly cold. After a good swim, unlike other extreme workouts, one will not experience the hunger that most of those who workout in a gym experience, after their workouts are completed. Swimming improves the body's oxygen use and promotes healthy lung function without overworking the heart. Ocean swimming can have certain benefits, such as cleaning infected cuts and, clearing up skin problems. The cardiovascular benefits will remain the same no matter where you swim.

Ancient 20's teaching points on SWIMMING:

- Water resistance is greater than air resistance because it makes the muscles work harder.

- Unlike other sports, your weight, age or fitness level is not an issue

- Helps combat the aging process

- Increases energy level

- Promotes proper breathing

- Stimulates blood circulation (lack of circulation is a leading cause in many diseases including diabetes)

- Is one of the primary preferred doctor's choices of physical therapy after major orthopedic surgeries

- Works every single small and big muscle in the body simultaneously

- Trims fat and enhances the overall physique of the body.

  Even if you just were to use your local swimming pool two times per week, you would see a big difference. This is as good as it gets in the exercise world without putting any pressure on your joints. Try signing up for a local swimming or water aerobics class. You will find that there are many people who don't know how to swim but they love getting in the water because it awakens the kid in them and gives them a workout as well.

Law Four

MINIMIZE YOUR BREAD INTAKE: "KUWAIT"

"Acorns were good until bread was found." ~Francis Bacon

One good thing about traveling is that you get to decipher the truth about what local Media has been putting out about many of the so-called "War Countries" and "Anti-American Countries". To date, the country where I have felt the most comfortable and safe has been The Kingdom of Kuwait. With all due respect, the Kuwait that everyone in America knows and the Kuwait that I have come to know are two totally different entities. Kuwait City (the capital of Kuwait) is very clean, beautiful and has a beach that runs along the entire city! If you wanted to go somewhere in your car, you had to start the car first to let your air conditioner run. Then you'd run back into the house, because it was SCORCHING HOT.

I had never experienced 115 degree weather. It is an experience that I will never forget. It was so hot that everyone came out in the evening when the sun went down. People laugh when I tell them that I cannot honestly recall the physical appearance of anyone who was not a part of my team, because it was always dark when everyone came out. They were always covered in their traditional clothing from head to toe. After our practices, the team would go to eat at places like Johnny Rockets, Fuddruckers, Chili's and Fridays (there are plenty of American restaurants in Kuwait).

One day after practice, the team's assistant coach Mohammed decided to take me out to eat at a local restaurant, instead of one of the American establishments where I was accustomed to eating. I asked, "Coach where are we going?" and he replied in his best English, "D, I take care of you. Don't worry *habibi*." Habibi is a popular Arabic term of endearment which means "baby." This was the first time in my life that I had tried Arabic food so I was a bit nervous. Upon ordering our food the waiter brought out "two big pans of freshly baked bread". I looked as if I had seen a ghost because I was sure that all of that bread was not meant for the two of us. But when the coach started to dig into it, my suspicions went away.

There was absolutely no way that any human being could eat this amount of bread and still have room for a meal. I ate so much bread that when the food came I could not take a single bite! Coach laughed at me because I was not yet broken in to this custom and the Arabic style of eating. When we left the restaurant I looked around me and noticed that many of the males had big stomachs after they ate. In fact, my stomach was bulging and I am a mere 6 feet 4 inches and 190 pounds.

In Kuwait and most Arabic countries bread is served before every meal! Sometimes they would just sit and eat bread with a side dish called "hummus" (Arabian dip made from chickpeas, olive oil, lemon juice, salt, and garlic). Before seeing the men's stomach bloat at the restaurant, I was well aware that your stomach would bloat a little after each meal. But, what I had seen was not the "normal after meal stomach inflation". I had eaten a significant amount of bread as a child but not at this rate. These gentlemen drove me to see what was behind the bread and how bread should be eaten.

Bread contains microorganisms called yeasts which are one-celled bacteria that reproduce rapidly. The reproduction process starts by dividing into two young yeasts rapidly and given the proper environmental conditions and enough sugar to eat, yeast can reproduce in five minutes or less and has the ability to give off carbon dioxide. After reading this I had an entire new view on bread. It does not take a rocket scientist to know that carbon dioxide is not something that should be ingested by humans in heavy doses. According to *Joy of cooking* "there are 200 billion yeast cells in an ounce of yeast. Due to its uncanny ability to reproduce itself in such a short period of time, only a small quarter ounce package of dry yeast is all it takes to make a one pound loaf of bread rise."

The *Whole Grains Council* officials encourage eating whole grain bread (100% wheat) because it has more vitamins and twice the fiber than white bread. This kind of bread is likely to be sold at a local organic store. Be mindful that pizza, crackers, cake, chicken nuggets, fish sticks and many other products around the house contain bread and some form of yeast.

When I was younger my mother used to make a lot of "Muffin Mix Cornbread" so I could eat it with my beans and turnip greens. After learning of what things are actually inside of the muffin mix, I decided to cut back on eating it, because I wanted to live a healthier lifestyle. If you are trying to lose weight, cutback on certain bread intake and you will noticeably drop pounds. White bread is a low-fiber starchy carbohydrate that you may want to consider avoiding, because this form of carbohydrate (i.e. white rice, processed grains, potatoes, etc) is more rapidly converted into simple sugars by your body. For many, this may seem like an impossible task, but the more you cut back, the more evident and rapid will be your results.

To understand how much bread you are consuming, read the back labels of all of the food that you consume.

If those labels contain; yeast, leavening agents, bread

crumbs, dough, or anything that is associated with rising agents, chances are you are eating bread. Once you read the labels and find out which products contain bread agents, try to go without eating those foods for about 7 days. The no bread-product fast will allow you to fully comprehend the amount of bread you unknowingly consume on a daily basis.

Law Five

DO NOT EAT 3 HOURS BEFORE YOU SLEEP: "GERMANY"

"Eat well, drink in moderation, and sleep sound. In these three, good health abound." ~Latin Proverb

My very first European contract came from the country which was very instrumental in shaping World History – Germany. Before arriving to Germany, I had no prior knowledge of the country, except old war footage from WWII. Germany was filled with U.S. military bases, which helped me relax in my new environment. In fact, Frankfurt, the city I arrived in could be compared to New York City. Both Frankfurt and New York are multi-cultural and in both places there are multiple activities with which to keep busy. There are many voluminous things I can say about Frankfurt. The place where I actually lived was called Cologne. In my mind, Cologne is much like a smaller version of Miami, in that there are a lot of activities taking place and the city never sleeps.

As a 23 year old, my eyes lit up when I saw what the night life of Cologne (or Koln) had to offer me. After being in Cologne for only 2 weeks, I was eager hit the club scene. The stage fright and shock of being away from home had finally begun to wear off. There were nights when I had a game the next day at 1 pm and I stayed out until 9 a.m. that morning. I have never used drugs and on average I consume wine less than three times per year, so my late nights were much easier on me than a few of my teammates.

I lived in a suburb of Cologne called Bergheim.

This meant that staying out late would be taking a risk on getting back home. Often times after leaving the night club, I had to sprint to the Hauptbahnhof (the train station) to catch the earliest train in order to get back to Bergheim so that I could get enough rest for practice or the game. I played a few games "on fumes" alone! In the midst of all of my hanging out, I ran across a German named Andres and we became friends. Andres was of Serbian decent but he was born in Germany. In Andres's mind he was Germany's answer to Fabio. Besides the sport of basketball, the one thing that Andres and I had in common is that we both appreciated the beauty of women. For these reasons and more, we got along really well. Spending time with Andres allowed me to learn more about "unwritten rules" of nightlife in Cologne. He helped me learn the ropes of Germany and treated me as a brother.

The one thing that he loved to do was lift weights. He would spend hours in the gym and take supplements to define his muscles. I would say Arnold Schwarzenegger had a huge impact on athletic training especially in Germany and Austria (Arnold's native country). After about 2 months of being in Germany, I noticed that I had not seen a change in Andres physically since he had been pounding the weights nonstop. I knew that he was putting in the hours in the gym but I could see any physical improvements over those 2 months. I soon found out the reason for his physical plateau. One night after leaving Club Watiza, we stopped at a small hamburger stand that was the "place of choice" to eat for all the night owls. Andres elected to eat two specially made hamburgers with toppings such as mayonnaise, onions, mustard, pickles and potatoes. I chose a to drink a freshly squeezed juice, the reason being that it was 4 a.m. in the morning and I knew I did not like eating that late.

Andres's inability to get his body in shape could be traced to his late night binge eating habits.

The issue at hand is that not only is it terrible to eat that late, but also the kind of food that is eaten at that hour is not nutritious. This brings me to the purpose of this chapter which is, "you cannot eat 3 hours before you go to bed", which is exactly what my friend was doing. All the gym work he was doing was in vain because he was canceling himself out because of the time he chose to eat and the type of food he ate. It is a known fact that most club goers or late night shift workers gain a bulk of their weight because of their hours of operation. The longer you stay up the more fuel your body is going to need to sustain a respectable energy level. If you are in bed resting at a decent hour, is it probable that you will be up in the wee hours eating hot dogs, ice cream, hamburgers, etc? Now you can understand how being healthy all ties together (see law two).

Ancient 20's teaching points on EATING THREE HOURS BEFORE YOU SLEEP:

- You can gain weight because your body is not at its full capacity and your digestive system will only work at 50% to breakdown food.

- Have trouble sleeping because your digestive organs stay up digesting food and it forces you to sleep on your stomach because your system is working overtime to compensate for the lack of "full cooperation" from other parts of the digestive system. This may affect the stomach causing internal injuries.

- Increase your risk for diseases. Most people that eat late at night and go to sleep are eating meals that have no nutritional value, what so ever. Most times it stems from fast food restaurants and something that is fried or cooked in a quick and unhealthy manner. Those foods are most commonly, French fries, hamburgers, hot dogs, etc.

By no means do I encourage going to sleep hungry, but I do recommend eating the right things that will help your body grow and heal. Under normal conditions, most nutritionist would tell you it is best to eat before 7:00 p.m. Of course, this is not conducive to everyone's lifestyle. Keeping this point in mind there are a few things that you can eat before sleep that will "get you through" the night.

Ancient 20's THREE ITEMS that you can eat before you sleep:

* *A handful of almonds* - Almonds contain tryptophan and magnesium that relaxes muscles. Tryptophan is an amino acid, which helps calm your mind and encourages sleep. Also, almonds have many other benefits for the body, because they contain phytochemicals, which are plant chemicals that may provide powerful protection against heart disease, stroke, and other chronic diseases.

* *Oatmeal* - Will stop hunger plus it is a source of soporific melatonin (which means sleep inducing hormones).

* *A cup of Chamomile Tea* - will relax the body so that you can sleep with great comfort.

The time that you eat is just as important, as what kind of food you eat. "When" determines "why" your body responds the way it does during the day. Drinking also applies in this instance, not just eating alone. To give you a final example, you would not drink two bottles of "an energy drink" hoping to go to sleep, because the entire purpose of any energy drink is to keep you awake and energized.

Law Six

UNNATURAL MILK DOES NOT DO THE BODY GOOD:
"SWEDEN"

"I don't believe that you have to be a cow to know what milk
is." ~Ann Landers

When travel is a big part of your job, you tend to miss
special holidays with your family. Due to my not being with
family during those holidays, I learned that much of the
world has the same customs and celebrations they just
recognize them in different ways. There was one occasion
when I went to Stockholm, Sweden to play and I had the
good fortune of arriving a day before the New Years day
celebration. Stockholm was a city rich in tradition and had
a classic European city feel to it. Needless to say, we
enjoyed ourselves the night of New Year's Eve and brought
in New Years Day on a positive note.

The next morning, in the hotel, I remember getting a
wakeup call (as a prank from my teammates) to eat
breakfast at about 7:00 am. When I arrived downstairs, I
saw that the breakfast was a mere piece of bread, under
cooked eggs and some milk! I looked at the waitress in my
best broken English and asked, "Is this all the food that you
have?" (Sometimes it was necessary for me to speak in
"broken English" because that was the only way they could
understand me).

She replied with a stern "no, this is the breakfast of choice
here in the hotel." I just shook my head and walked away
in disappointment.

I then went to McDonald's (which had to be to this day the most expensive McDonald's I have ever frequented) and ordered a small breakfast.

In fact, the food was so high priced that I had to borrow some 'Swedish Krona' (their currency) from a teammate named Brandon. He always finds time to remind me of how he took care of me during our time in Stockholm. While eating my food in the restaurant, I noticed the same thing that I saw back in the hotel. Everyone had a glass of milk, as a part of their breakfast. I know in America we drink milk, but in Sweden they drink milk like we drink water. I started to believe that maybe it was true that milk does the body good. Allow me to inform you that "my milk hypothesis" was tossed right out of the window. After about 4 days in Sweden, I had noticed that there were many elder citizens who had deformed bone structure problems such as hunch back, knee problems, foot problems, and many other health issues. Upon looking at the number of countries that consume milk, I found that Sweden was second in the world, behind Finland, in per capita for milk consumption. Sweden averaged 145.5 liters per capita. This number may not sound like a lot but consider that the United States finished with a 89.4 liter per capita rating that year! It is also notable that Denmark, Norway, Holland, and Sweden have the highest rates of *breast cancer* in the world. Ironically, they also had the highest rates of *osteoporosis,* as well. It is because of their high milk consumption. What this means is that milk is not as good for the body, as one may have been lead to believe. I will not venture to say that ALL milk is not healthy, but I will say that being without milk will not hurt you in any way.

According to Robert Cohen, author of *Milk The Deadly Poison,* sixty percent of cows in America have "Leukemia Virus", and eighty percent have what is known as "Para tuberculosis."

Para tuberculosis causes *Irritable Bowel Syndrome,* which affects 4 million American women. Another interesting fact is there are 4,000 mammals with over 500,000 hormones, but the irony in this is that, only one growth hormone in all of nature between two mammals are identical and that hormone is between human and cow. The captivating part is this same growth hormone can be found in milk! This hormone is the most powerful growth hormone in the human body. If you are a person with cancer and drinking milk daily, you have just "DOUBLED" the only hormone that makes breast cancer grow.

Cohen goes on to say that "the number one protein in milk is called casein. Eighty percent of the protein in milk is the same in the glue that they use to put a label on a bottle of beer. The same glue that holds your wooden furniture together, is also derived from this very same protein. So, in essence you are drinking glue." The greatest controversy in the history of the FDA is the genetic engineering of milk. Did you know that protein inhibits calcium absorption? Milk is nothing more than liquid protein. You can get your calcium intake from "leafy green vegetables", so it is not mandatory that you drink milk to have strong bones like so many of us have believed for so long.

Here are three facts for you to consider. Fact one: The food that newborn mammals receive from their mothers is extremely necessary for its survival. When they are grown, mammals stop drinking milk and follow other diets. An adult cow will die from its' mother's milk. Conscious doctors will tell a woman to breastfeed their children up until 2 years, if it does not cause her too much discomfort. Maternal milk is very healthy, tasty and nutritious, when it comes from our own species. We are, however, the only species who continues to drink milk, well into our adult years. Fact two: Cow pus, mucous, and "snot" are all in milk, but it is very difficult to fully eradicate all of the bacteria. Surprisingly, the FDA still allows companies to sell it.

Fact three: According to the U.S. Department of Health and Human Services, lactose intolerance is affecting 95 percent of Asians, 60 to 80 percent of African-Americans and Ashekenazi Jews, 80 to 100 percent of American Indians and 50 to 80 percent of Hispanics. If you are lactose intolerant, this alone, is a red flag of your body, screaming at you that you should not drink milk or consume any dairy products. These products all stem from milk. Your body has built-in mechanisms to alert you, if something is going wrong with your body. Most of us have a tendency to ignore what our body is trying to tell us. Here is a point to consider. If you are driving and the check engine light comes on in your car, would you knock the light out and continue driving for days or months without getting it checked out? Of course you wouldn't. That is what you are doing to your body when you eat or drink something and your stomach doesn't agree with it but you consume it anyway. Stay alert and watch for the body's signs. Pain is a good thing because it lets you know that something is wrong and it needs to be fixed.

God created man as a perfect being who has the capability of healing himself by ad hearing to a proper diet, one rich in natural nutrients and minerals of the earth.

Law Seven

WHY THE SUDDEN HYPE OVER BOTTLED WATER?
"PUERTO RICO"

"Water is the most neglected nutrient in your diet but one of
the most vital." ~Kelly Barton

I stressed earlier in Law One, the importance of drinking
water for good health. This Journey will focus on the
differences between drinking bottled water and drinking
water from the tap. In December of 1997, my college
basketball team got invited to the San Juan Shootout in San
Juan, Puerto Rico. This was a tournament where many big
universities from across the United States came and played
against each other, including one or two teams from Puerto
Rico.

All of the University's students were at home over Christmas
break for a month, so our campus was a ghost town. All we
did was practice, practice and did I mention practice? So
you could imagine that every player on the team looked
forward to going to Puerto Rico. It would be viewed as a
paid vacation for the entire team. This was the first time
that I traveled to another country that was not accessible
from the United States by car. We stayed in the "Condado
Hotel", located directly on the Atlantic Ocean. This hotel
was extremely nice. A clean beach that was second to none,
nice restaurants, a casino and top of the line customer

service were just a few of the amenities that were a part of the hotel. As somewhat of a risk taker I was more intrigued with the hotel casino. I was only 19 years old and this was the first time that I had been allowed access inside of a real casino.

I can remember my coach sitting everyone down and giving us a lecture that we should stay away from the casinos and get some rest. This was like telling a man NOT to look at a beautiful woman when she walks by. It's not going to happen! Coach's encouragement lecture went in and out of everyone's ears faster than it takes a light to turn on at the flip of the switch. Soon enough, I found myself in the casino with my teammate, Nehemiah Dannes. We were having the times of our lives. As these times went on, I started to lose quite a bit of money and the time of my life started to turn into a nightmare. It got so bad that I started going to the ATM machine to withdraw money that the university had given me as food allowance! If I could have used the elastic from my underwear as a form of currency I would have. All of my meal money was gone, so I had to pull out all stops in a last ditch effort to finish on top. More than a decade has passed and I'm still waiting on that comeback. Needless to say, I became just another statistic who thought that they could beat the casino and lost. After I lost every form of currency that I owned, I figured it was time for something to eat. Nehemiah and I went to grab a bite to eat in the casino on a food voucher that I had won in the casino. Before ordering our meals we asked the waiter for water.

The waiter returned with "two bottles of water, in hand." Receiving bottled water in a restaurant was unusual to me, as I was used to drinking normal tap water. So, I asked the waiter, if he could bring us regular water in a glass.

He looked at me in shock, as if I had demanded from him one million dollars in small bills in an offshore account in the Cayman Islands. He told us that he would not drink water from the tap even to save his life. This put us in a state of fear and we took the bottled waters. I did realize that we were in a country not of our own so I did not want to take the risk of drinking filthy water. But why was the waiter so adamant about not drinking tap water? After all I had seen many local elderly Puerto Ricans and I'm sure not every one of them drank water from the tap and they seemed to have turned out just fine.

When he returned he told us that we are nearing the 21st century and no one drinks tap water anymore because it is not healthy for you. This was the first I'd heard of tap water not being healthy. After all, I drank tap water up to this point in my life and I never had a single illness from it. More importantly, why hadn't anyone told me about this bottled water revolution? Surely it had to be important if the bottled water supposedly gave us supreme health? After returning back to the United States, I found that bottled water had been marketed all across the world in an effort to improve health and provide us with cleaner water. As time went along, I had seen that it was not so much about "our health" as it was about "making money" and creating another fear mechanism for citizens. After all how could people in the 1800's and 1900's drink water from the tap (or rivers and lakes) and be perfectly fine but all of a sudden drinking water from the tap in your house makes you get sick?

Naturally, water in some countries may be unhealthy due to their irrigation system and safety regulation guidelines. If you are currently drinking water from the tap, do not feel ashamed. Some bottled water may present a health threat to people with weakened immune systems such as cancer patients and those that have HIV or AIDS. The reason is that the HHS (U.S. Department of Health and Human Services) has no standards that require bottled water to be any better than tap water.

A big part of the issue may be that "bottled water" and "tap water" are regulated by two separate entities.

According to the HHS, *"Bottled water and tap water are regulated by two different agencies: FDA regulates bottled water and the Environmental Protection Agency (EPA) regulates tap water, also referred to as municipal water or public drinking water. EPA's Office of Ground Water and Drinking Water has issued extensive regulations on the production, distribution and quality of public drinking water, including regulations on source water protection, operation of drinking water systems, contaminant levels, and reporting requirements. However, the FDA regulates bottled water as a food."*

EPA officials have stated that tap water contains "toxins" such as: chlorine, lead, and other chemicals that gets into the water supply. The truth of the matter is that tap water does indeed contain certain elements and chemicals that are harmful to the body, but it also contains some minerals that the body requires. In the early 1900's, the world was not as advanced as it is now and I can tell you that many people lived longer lives without bottled water. While researchers will tell you that the average life span a few hundred years ago were shorter, what they don't tell you is that it was ONLY shorter due to infant mortality. Many children died during birth and hence the average life span was cut down but as an overall average they lived longer lives. If someone lived to be 100 years of age and then comes a child who dies in childbirth, the average life span is divided between those two and is cut down to 50 years.

As a child growing up, I was lead to believe that: tin, lead, titanium, arsenic, chromium and aluminum were all things that should never be consumed by humans. Some of these elements can be found in tap water. However, all of the aforementioned elements are actually "trace minerals" that we must consume to stave off deficiency diseases. They could be toxic if given in unsafe doses. I once seen a television special years ago that said, "Most bottled water is not even fit to do your dishes in." Economically speaking the world could save money by cutting down on the manufacturing of bottled water because bottled water, ounce for ounce, cost more than gas.

Below is a comparison chart done by the *Community Water Company of Green Valley.* You may find the results astonishing.

Tap Water	Bottled Water
Regulated by EPA	Regulated by FDA
Cannot have confirmed E. coli or fecal Coli form bacteria.	A certain amount of any bacteria is allowed.
Filtered and/or disinfected	No federal filtration or disinfection requirements.
Violation of drinking water standards are grounds for enforcement.	Bottled water in violation of standards can still be sold.
Utilities must have their water tested by certified labs.	Such testing is not required for bottlers.
Tap water results must be reported to state or federal officials.	There are no reporting requirements for bottlers.
Water system operators must be certified.	Bottled water plant operators do not have to be certified.
Water suppliers must issue consumer confidence reports annually.	There are no public right-to-know requirements for bottlers.
Costs pennies a day	Costs $.80 to $4.00 per gallon.
Contains essential nutrients for the body such as calcium and iron.	Natural minerals are removes by filtration.
Chlorine residual in water to prevent bacteria growth.	No disinfectant present to kill bacteria in bottles

I was compelled to share this journey because tap water has gotten such a bad reputation over the last decade. I am not saying that one is better than the other, but the statistics do speak for themselves. There are several bottled water companies that take the time to provide premier quality drinking water.

If you desire to take a simpler route, you can buy a water filtration device for your home. This would allow you to use water from the tap, and filter the unwanted microbes from the tap water. I personally prefer this method because it is the most economical. When shopping for a filtration system, be sure that it contains a pore size efficiency of less than 0.4 microns. If the pore size is bigger than 0.4 microns, it may not be effective in removing protozoa such as Cryptosporidium and Giardia.

As you continue to purchase bottled water please make sure to look on the label to ensure that the water has undergone the "reverse osmosis" process.

Always check the bottle before purchasing and ask questions if no labels are present. If it does not say reverse osmosis on the label, then it would not be the best option, as far as drinking water is concerned. Contrary to popular belief, not all bottled water is good for you.

Law Eight

IF YOU MUST FRY FOODS, USE OLIVE OIL: "TURKEY"

"I come bearing an olive branch in my hand, and the
freedom fighter's gun in the other. Do not let the olive
branch fall from my hand." ~Yasser Arafat

As a pre-cursor, allow me to say that I do not recommend
eating fried foods. However, I understand that we live in a
world where everyone has a personal choice in how they
live. I realize that not everyone will give up fried foods
because they have grown accustomed to eating them for so
many years. It is with that in mind that this chapter was
written. The human species is imperfect. Now let's begin
our journey to Turkey.

I have always felt the further you continue to travel east in
the world from the United States, the less Americanized
those countries will be. It was not more evident to me than
when I arrived to Turkey (which bordered Iran, Iraq, and
Syria). The life in the east seems to be more old fashioned
and slower paced than life in the west. I say this because I
was spoiled by having the opportunity to work in the
Western European Countries for the first few years of my
career.

I have to say that God has a great love for me because he
did not send me to any remote Turkish city. He sent me to
live in Istanbul and Izmir. I worked in Turkey on two
separate occasions. Istanbul has the largest population in
Turkey (12.6 million people).

so holds the world's fourth largest population
: number three ranking in Europe, for
.n areas. Izmir, on the other hand, is
comparative to Los Angeles's weather and palm tree
scenery. The city has a population of 4 million people
ranking second to Istanbul for Turkey's biggest cities.

My favorite time in Turkey was playing for a club called
Tuborg Pilsener. Tuborg is a big beer company in Turkey
with factories and employees across Europe. The Club
leased apartments for foreign players and supplied us with
our own cars. In my spare I watched cable, played video
games and frequently visited the nearby shopping mall,
which is where I did my grocery shopping also. After getting
a feel for the landscape I decided to go to most famous
Turkish supermarket called Milagros, to see what kinds of
food I could buy that would be compatible with my body and
taste. One night, after practice I had my teammate drop me
off at the supermarket because I had a taste for some fried
chicken wings. I asked a young lady who was working at
the store, in which aisle the cooking oil could be found.
Because of the language barrier, she could not explain
exactly where it was shelved. Instead, she took me to the
aisle and handed me a bottle of "olive oil". I explained to her
that I was looking for oil to fry chicken, not olive oil. She
insisted that "this is what we (the Turks) use to fry our
food." After about 4 minutes of similar verbal exchanges, I
purchased the olive oil.

Frying chicken with olive oil would be new for me. I was a
bit skeptical of the oil since the only oils that we used in my
house to fry foods were Canola, Vegetable, or other corn
oils. The young lady made mention of vegetable oils that I
could have used but at that point I was sold on trying
something new.

In line with the saying *When in Rome do as the Romans do*, I decided since in Turkey, I'd fry chicken in olive oil, as many of the Turks do.

The chicken was cooked to a golden brown perfection color. I also noticed that while frying in olive oil, unlike other oils, the olive oil remained clear. Most oils leave the frying pan full of batter or flour, but with olive oil the flour actually stuck to the chicken!

Generally, olive oil is more expensive than shortening, vegetable or corn oil. In fact it's three times as costly, as the other oils, but "you get what you pay for." Olive oil is extremely delicate and has many beneficial health properties.

Studies conducted by the *International Olive Oil Council,* on healthy patients with gastro duodenal problems (gastritis, ulcer, liver and biliary complaints) reveal that there is no relationship between food fried in olive oil and these illnesses. The Council goes on to say that olive oil is ideal for frying. In proper temperature conditions, without over-heating, it undergoes no substantial structural change and keeps its nutritional value better than other oils. The antioxidants and oleic acid contained in olive oil, helps the oil preserve its health benefits. Oleic acid is an omega nine fatty acid that is considered to be one of the healthier sources of fat in the diet. Olive oil's high smoking point (410 F) is substantially higher than the ideal temperature for frying food (356 F). The fats with lower critical points, such as "corn" and "butter" break down at this temperature and form toxic products!

The consumption of olive oil also produces beautiful skin and also promotes cardiovascular health. It is a secret ingredient to having beautiful and shiny hair. Moroccan and North African women have known of this secret for hundreds of years.

The 3 common types of Olive oil are:

- Extra Virgin – This is the least processed and comes from the first pressing of the olives. Extra virgin, by far, is the best of the three. By best I mean the purest quality.

- Virgin Pure – Goes through some processing, filtering and refining. Considered second best.

- Extra Light – This oil has been heavily refined, has a pale color and minimal flavor. Also this particular oil's ingredients are not regulated by governing bodies in many countries so the flavor could vary. The intriguing fact about extra light oil is that it has a lower smoking point than the other two which make it more suitable to cook.

Olive oil is a dynamic element. More independent research will reveal additional benefits that can be used. For now, you know that olive oil is one of the "LESSER EVILS" when it comes to frying foods. However, frying foods should not be an option for ANYONE who seeks supreme health. Nobel Prize Nominee Dr. Joel Wallach warns against using any kind of oils for cooking. He recommends using butter at low temperatures. He goes on to say that if you eliminate fried foods completely from your diet, you could potentially add 25 years to your life (*See Dr. Wallach, Dead Doctors Don't Lie*). The reason is that once you open ANY bottle of cooking oil, that oil immediately starts to go rancid because it is in contact with the air. Once oxygen hits the oil, it starts to create free radicals which are notorious for causing cancers. Even worse, once you heat up the oil, start cooking animal fats, heating up sugars and other ingredients, the effects only multiply. If you put the oil in the refrigerator the oil will still go rancid, it will just do so at a slower pace than if it was left in the kitchen cabinet or elsewhere.

Other reasons why you should avoid frying

In 1997 The Harvard School of Public Health did a study that showed that the people of the Southeastern part of the United States have a lifespan that is shorter than the people in the upper Midwest. Do you know how the people who live in the upper Midwest prepare their food? They eat most of their food stewed, roasted, boiled and poached. The people who live in the Southeast part of the country (between Washington D.C. and East Texas) primarily eat fried foods such as fried fish, fried chicken, country fried steak, fried tomatoes, fried okra, fried potatoes and things of this nature. The fried food is the reason that their average life span is twenty years shorter than those who live in the upper Midwestern part of the country. The biggest sources of free radicals are margarines, cooking oils and fried foods. Simply put, heart disease, the prevention of heart disease and possibly the reversal of certain heart ailments can happen by totally eliminating free radicals from the diet. Our ancestors outlived us because they were cooking with creams and lard. Cardiomyopathy is a very important heart disease that you can sometimes survive. The flipside to surviving this disease is that doctors will have to put in a pacemaker or a stint and put you on drugs to control the rhythm of your heart.

Again, this chapter was put together for those who may not be as disciplined enough to go without ever eating fried foods again. Many people fry with vegetable oils. They may have heard about Olive oil but might not understand the components of Olive oil and what functions it serves as being 'The Lesser of Evils' of the other oils in terms of cooking.

Law Nine

SUBSTITUTE TRAIL MIX FOR JUNK FOOD: "CZECH REPUBLIC"

"No man in this world has more courage than the man who can stop after eating one peanut." ~Channing Pollock

Anyone who has ever held a job can certainly tell you there are ups and downs on the job. Professional athletes are no exception to that rule. I had an offer to play with a team in Grudziaz, Poland. The offer was good but had provisions that were not convenient for me as a player. I decided to take the risk and accept the contract. I left one team from San Cristobal, Dominican Republic to fly to Warsaw, Poland. This was the first time that I was ever involved with a flight that had 3 layovers. My flight took me from Santo Domingo, Dominican Republic transferred me to Madrid, Spain to Copenhagen, Denmark and finally to Warsaw, Poland.

Can you imagine how I felt after the flight? Then, after arriving in Warsaw, I was driven 4 hours to Grudziaz, the city in which I was to play. I was exhausted, but there was little time for rest; practice started the next day. When I got to practice, my teammates informed me that the coach was on "the hot seat" and we had to win the next game or he would be leaving. After hearing this, I already knew that I would be in for an experience I wouldn't forget while in Poland.

Unfortunately, we lost that game and sure enough, the coach was relieved of his duties immediately.

Actually he was not necessarily relieved of his duties, but he was "nudged to resign." Within two days there was a new coach, an accomplished coach from Greece who seemed to be very confident in his abilities to improve team play. Even though this coach was always smiling, there was something that did not sit well with me about my future in the team. His smile was more of a smokescreen to make you feel comfortable with him while there were more sinister things unfolding behind closed doors. When a player has an uneasy feeling and has no guaranteed contract, it makes for very rocky circumstances. This is where my contract comes into play.

In Poland, like most European countries, the tryout period was 14 days. Some players are lucky enough to get 7 day tryout periods (everything depends on how good your agent is). If the management was pleased with my performance during the Tryout Period, I was guaranteed a contract for the remainder of the season. Under normal circumstances, I would have no problem with this. But my developing problem came from the issue, that the coach who brought me in to the team had just left the team. So there I was, in tryout, for a coach who does not know me and I did not have the same contract security, as was the case for all the other players who had come before me. I admit that as a younger player I had a short fuse. I noticed that the coach had a great relationship with the European player at my position because they had played against each other before. The favoritism was evident from the start, so I decided to have a talk with the coach and I informed him that I was leaving the team because I had other obligations. I called up my brother-in-law, who was in the Czech Republic at the time (under a basketball contract as well) and I explained to him what was going on and he encouraged me to come and stay with him for a time until I secured another contract in Europe. So off to Brno, Czech Republic I went.

As I de-boarded the airplane in Prague, I realized that I was very hungry since I had not eaten anything before leaving Warsaw. One thing I never do in any country is just "jump right into their cuisine," before doing a little research about the foods. If you have ever traveled you know that most airport food is comprised of potato chips, candy bars, fast foods and other non nutritional vittles. When you don't speak the native language of a particular country, you tend to move along as smoothly as you can, without asking questions or disrupting anyone. I entered a shop that sold all kinds of things to eat (half of which I knew nothing about) and I saw a package called "studentenfutter". It appeared to be a host of food items all mixed together in one bag. The only word I could make out on the package was "student." Studentenfutter is the German word for "trail mix" which translates directly as *student feed*. The trail mix, contained a healthy combination of natural foods and served as an excellent source of energy for both thinkers and athletes.

I found the trail mix to be extremely fulfilling and very tasteful. I was really in awe of what it did for me. In fact EVERYTIME that I travel now I bring 2 to 3 bags of trail mix along and stash them in my computer bag. For those of you who like to snack a lot during the day, this is the perfect snack. This snack satisfies your hunger in a healthy way. The common ingredients found in most trail mixes have been carefully broken down for you to see.

Ancient 20's facts on TRAILMIX INGREDIENTS:

- *Walnuts* – Helps, to support the immune system through an antioxidant called *ellagic acid*. Walnuts are also relatively high in L-Arginine, an essential amino acid that is converted in your body to *Nitric Oxide*. Nitric Oxide helps keep the inner walls of your blood vessels smooth and allows blood vessels to relax.

- *Peanuts* – Are considered a vegetable but they contain *resveratol* beneficial in protecting a person's body from cancer and viruses. It also acts as a anti-inflammatory that can help slow down the aging process and promote longevity. You can also find resveratol in red grapes.

- *Cashews* – Help maintain healthy gums and teeth. It also helps the body utilize iron, eliminate free radicals, develop bone and connective tissue, and produce the hair and skin pigment melanin. Cashews have no cholesterol.

- *Cranberries* - Contains what we call *Proanthocyanidins* that can inhibit bacteria from attaching to the wall of the urinary tract. This limits their ability to produce colonies and spread infection.

- *Almonds* – Are rich in *phytochemicals* which are plant components that promote heart and vascular health. A handful of almonds is a leading source of vitamin E and magnesium and offers protein, potassium, calcium, phosphorus and iron.

- *Raisins* – Are rich in *boron.* Boron is essential for bone health and prevention of osteoporosis. Moreover, it is vital for the absorption of the other minerals particularly calcium, magnesium and phosphorus and for maintaining health levels of minerals in the body.

- *Pumpkinseeds* – Are a great source of prostate support for males. They contain the chemical substances known as *cucurbitacins* that can prevent your body from converting testosterone into a much more potent form of this hormone called *dihydrotestosterone.* With dihydrotestosterone, it is more difficult for your body to produce more prostate cells, which is better for your prostate health.

- *Sunflowers* – Assists memory and cognitive function, through its content of *choline*.

- *Pecans* – Are 53 percent fat by weight, 29 of the 47 grams of fat contained in one serving is in the form of mostly monosaturated fat oleic acid (which we discussed in the chapter about milk). Pecans are also a dietary source of fiber, vitamin E, copper and magnesium.

For those who are struggling with digestive tract issues, it behooves you to make trail mix an integral part in your diet. Trail mix is also one of the most recommended foods that you should eat during, or before, a full body cleanse. Eating trail mix is a sure fire way of improving digestion while at the same time allowing you to shed unwanted pounds and dispel toxins.

Law Ten

CHOOSE HONEY AS A SWEETENER NOT SUGAR:
"MEXICO"

"And John himself was clothed in camel's hair, with a leather belt around his waist; and his food was locusts and wild honey." ~Matthew 3:4

It was a gut-wrenching and extremely rocky flight from Denver, Colorado to El Paso, Texas. No one confessed aloud but we all were secretly thanking the father up above for getting us to Texas safely. From the El Paso airport, we took a charter bus in to Juarez, Mexico. We arrived in Juarez the night before our first playoff game. El Paso borders Juarez, so you can pretty much walk into Mexico from Texas. This was my first time being in Mexico, so my interest was piqued well before I had arrived because I had heard so many tales of the dangers of some of the cities in Mexico. At this time, I was a member of the Fresno Heatwave, of the American Basketball Association (ABA). The Heatwave originated in Fresno, California.

The ABA served as a training ground for basketball players aspiring to play in the National Basketball Association (NBA). My first evening in Juarez, some teammates and I decided to go to a local diner to eat. I played it safe, and ordered 3 beef, soft-shelled tacos and some green tea. I had a custom before most games to drink tea the night before which always seemed to give me energy and relax me.

At my request, the waitress brought me the tea after the meal was finished.

I once had an athletic trainer who always said that drinking during the meal takes away from your enjoyment of the food, because you will be full before you finish your meal. After the waitress set down my cup she went back to the kitchen and came out with a bottle of honey. I asked her why she had left a bottle of honey on the table and she stated in Spanish "es mejor si bebes el te con la miel que con el azucar," which means "It is better to drink tea with honey than with sugar."

The idea of drinking tea with honey made me laugh. Up until this point I had only eaten honey with my biscuits. Prior to my visit to Juarez, sugar was my preferred sweetener in tea and all other drinks. She then stated that "El Americano tiene la cabeza tan duro, y cree que su manera es la unica manera de lograr cosas en la vida." When I heard her say this I took the bottle of honey and poured it into my cup in an effort to prove her wrong, but it turned out that I was the one who was sorely mistaken. What she had told me was, "The American has a very hard head and believes that his way is the only way to do things in life." This provoked me to "show her up" as I would put it, but my course of action failed, because the taste was very good. When she saw the look on my face, she started to laugh and nod her head, as if to say "I told you so." She went on to say that honey was much better for our bodies than sugar, because sugar does the body harm and honey helps the body in many ways. Secondly, this was the form of "sweetener" that was used in her village because of its mind boggling health benefits.

After drinking another cup of tea with honey, I was at least convinced that honey WAS a better tasting sweetener than sugar. What I had to do then was my due diligence on the health benefits of choosing honey instead of granulated sugar.

Through my research, I learned that honey does not contain table sugar *per se* but it does get its sweetness from monosaccharides, fructose and glucose and has approximately the same relative sweetness as granulated sugar. Honey is comprised of minerals such as copper, iodine, zinc, potassium, calcium, magnesium and sulfur. It also contains vitamins B1, B2, C, B6, B5 and B3 the levels of which change according to the qualities and sources of the nectar and pollen.

According to Dr. Jennifer Daniels author of the audio lecture, *Slave Quarter Cures*, "White sugar when not accompanied by B-Vitamins and minerals enters your body and pulls fluids from all over your body dehydrating your organs and pulling B-Vitamins from the brain making you forgetful while also pulling minerals from your bones giving you osteoporosis."

Based on research from *Bees-Online* and *Thomas Honey Company*, here are *10 benefits* that honey can provide:

- Can be used instead of alpha hydroxyl acid beauty masks because of its high content of AHA acid.

- Can be used as hair conditioner when mixed with Olive Oil.

- Can be used as a natural antiseptic for cuts because it contains chemicals that kill fungi.

- May be effective in helping cure ulcers.

- Accelerates skin healing. Since the "sugar-like substance" in honey absorbs water it helps to trap some of the moisture to prevent bacteria and other microbes from growing as easily as in other food.

- Serves as a good source of antioxidants.

- Easily digested to help kidneys and intestines function better.

- Rapidly diffuses through the blood. When accompanied by warm water, honey diffuses into the blood stream in 7 minutes. Its free sugar-like molecules make the brain function better since the brain is the largest consumer of sugar, therefore, reduces fatigue.

- Helps to sooth cough.

- Supports blood formation by cleansing the blood. It also functions as a protection against capillary problems and arteriosclerosis.

  Now that you know the benefits of honey, let's learn the harm that sugar does to our bodies. Nancy Appleton, PhD and author of *"Lick The Sugar Habit"* has a few interesting findings about sugar.

  Sugar can:

- Lead to alcoholism.

- Throws off the body's homeostasis (which means the condition of the body to seek a condition of balance).

- Subdue your immune system and impair your defenses against infectious disease.

- Upset the mineral relationships in your body causing chromium, vanadium and copper deficiencies and interferes with absorption of calcium and magnesium.

- Produce a significant rise in total cholesterol and triglycerides.

- Contribute to and cause appendicitis, varicose veins, gallstones, hemorrhoids and food allergies.

- Increase fasting levels of glucose and can cause reactive hypoglycemia.

- Cause drowsiness and decreased activity in children.

- Increase the size of your liver by making your liver cells divide and it can increase the amount of liver fat.

- Be higher in people with Parkinson's disease.

Appleton goes on to list many more facts about sugar that affect the human body in a negative way. It is understood that sugar is a big part of most of our lives. We can change the way in which we intake sugar, by changing the actual "sugar source" when we want something to be sweeter. The evidence of what the honey will do for you will be in the way you feel after a few weeks. Knowing the benefits of honey may be especially beneficial for someone who is diabetic.

In departing, I wish to inform you about "artificial sweeteners." Many people use artificial sweeteners while believing that they are making the healthier choice. I will not name call but many sweeteners claim to replace the sugar taste without actually giving you "the sugar". Steer clear of these because they have been known to have serious health repercussions. Besides honey, another safe natural sweetener is actually known as *STEVIA*. Stevia, is a plant primarily grown in Paraguay and Brazil. Stevia is made by crushing or distilling, the leaves of the plant to a powder or syrup. If you should choose to use Stevia, remember to use only a small amount, as it is sweeter than other sweeteners.

Law Eleven

NEVER EAT UNLESS YOU ARE HUNGRY: "CHINA"

"My doctor told me to stop having intimate dinners for four, unless there are three other people." ~Orson Welles

The closest I had ever been to China, was ordering a large side of chicken fried rice from our local Chinese restaurant back home in Detroit. That all changed when I received a call back, in 2001, to go to China. I was picked to play a few exhibition games against some of the best players of the Chinese local league called the Chinese Basketball Association (CBA). The trip was to last 15 days in which we were scheduled to play 12 games against different teams in the Chinese league. It was a process, in and of itself, just to organize travel arrangements to fly to China. My passport and birth certificate had to be sent to New York, to the Chinese Consular's office, to acquire a visa for travel. Once I received my visa, I had to catch a flight from Detroit then Los Angeles, because team officials had booked everyone's departing flight together from the Los Angeles Airport (LAX). I later found out that this way was the fastest route.

The flight from Los Angeles to China was the longest flight of my life. It took 13 hours to get to China! In spite of the long and restless flight the airline stewardesses did a great job of ensuring that all the players were comfortable. We arrived in Shanghai without any problem or issues. The service there was first class. When we arrived, the shuttle buses were waiting for us. After we arrived at the hotel, everyone was assigned a roommate and we all got settled in. I must say the shock of seeing "my toilet in the ground" was enough to make me not want to use my bathroom. Yes, you heard me loud and clear, IN THE GROUND WITH FOOT PRINTS. It was certainly an adventure!

As we traveled to Beijing, I learned that not every hotel was equipped with in the ground toilets. In Beijing, things were much closer to, what I was used to as it was somewhat more westernized. On the other hand, the "Chinese food" was not the same type of Chinese food that, I had eaten at home in Detroit. On the menu were: shark fin cake, whole fried duck, and other things that I could barely pronounce. They did have rice but it was always white rice with mixed in scrambled eggs. They informed me that the Chinese restaurants in Europe and the United States had to tailor their style of cooking to fit the need of the customer so most Chinese restaurants outside of China were not serving 100% Chinese cuisine.

Most of the time, I found myself eating at McDonald's and Kentucky Fried Chicken except, when I attended the mandatory team dinners. Eating fast food was not my regular diet, but it was the better of the two choices.

Getting around in China would not be the easiest thing to do if you could not speak the language. However, my roommate and I had a translator who walked around with us to make sure we could get everything we needed and that no one would try to harm us in any way. We called him Mr. Chen. I could not pronounce his first name so we called him by his last name. He was a young man who had studied English and was extremely intelligent.

Mr. Chen would take us anywhere that we wanted to go and he would not complain but something was strange about him that I eventually noticed.

There was one particular day that my roommate decided to sleep in, so Chen came to get me at 10 o'clock in the morning. I went shopping to buy DVDs (10 for $5). At that time, the Chinese Yen was 8 to 1, meaning for $1.00 I could get 8 Chinese Yen. I bought about 50 DVDs. Afterwards Chen took me to Pizza Hut to eat. This was a relief for me. As I ate, Chen sat there and conversed with me just as he always did, but it had dawned on me that Chen would pass the entire day with us and he never ate!

I thought nothing of it the first few times but then I asked him, "Chen, why don't you ever eat?" He said "Because I am never hungry until the night time". I then proceeded to tell him that he needed to eat something throughout the day to carry him through so that he could have sufficient energy in order to function properly. He came back with "Here in China we do not eat just to eat, we eat to replenish our bodies and satisfy our hunger. In your country the people eat because they are programmed to eat at certain times of the day whether they are hungry or not. You eat late in the night and you wake up early in the morning to eat without a real hunger." I had to think about what he said and I realized that he was correct. I was told by so many health experts that "eating 4 or 5 small meals a day" was the right thing to do and that "breakfast is the most important meal of the day."

Could those statements be nothing more than marketing gimmicks? If you think about it logically, why would you eat anything if you were not hungry? That would honestly be insane, but it is something that many people do daily.

The late Wallace Wattles stated in his book, *"The Science of Being Well"* that "the processes of digestion and assimilation are under the supervision and control of an inner division of man's mentality,which are generally called the sub-conscious mind. We must not fail, however, to make the clear distinction between hunger and appetite. Hunger is the call of the sub-conscious mind for more material to be used in repairing and renewing the body and keeping up the internal heat; and hunger is never felt unless there is a need for more material and unless there is power to digest it when taken into the stomach".

Wattles goes on to say that, the "Appetite is a desire for the gratification of sensation. The drunkard has an appetite for liquor but he cannot have a hunger for it. A normally fed person cannot have a hunger for candy or sweets; the desire for these things is an appetite".

Essentially most of the time we are not hungry we just have appetites for things like I had for fried chicken wings, while living in Turkey. We have brought about health problems because of a simple *"want"* for something not a *"need"* for nourishment. Reread the statements by Mr. Wattles, so that you can fully understand the origins of your eating habits and how to correct them. The lemon pound cake, candy bar and ice cream are all things that you have an appetite for but are not things that your body needs.

Wattles also touched on a key fact that Mr. Chen spoke to me about while I was in China – breakfast. We as Americans love to gorge for breakfast, when in actuality how can we wake up and be hungry from doing nothing but resting?

Wattles says:

"There is no such possible thing as a normal or genuine hunger after arising from sound sleep. *The early morning breakfast is always taken to gratify appetite, never to satisfy hunger.* No matter whom you are or what your condition is; no matter how hard you work, or how much you are exposed, *unless you go to bed starved,* you cannot arise from your bed hungry. Hunger is not caused by sleep, but by work.

And it does not matter who you are, what your condition, or how hard or easy your work, the so-called no-breakfast plan is the right plan for you. It is the right plan for everybody because it is based on the universal law that hunger never comes until it is EARNED."

Let's be mindful to take the time to really ask ourselves, "Am I really hungry?" before our next meal.

Law Twelve

KEEP A BOTTLE OF OREGANO OIL IN YOUR CABINET:
"ESTONIA"

"Oregano is the spice of life."   ~Henry J. Tillman

The time is roughly 6:30 A.M. and I am not feeling well because I had a slight fever. The unfortunate part is that my flight was to leave in less than 2 hours from Detroit Metro Airport to Tallinn, Estonia, part of the former republic of Russia. Before this trip, I could not tell you where Estonia was located, so this was sure to be an educational experience that I would surely remember. My flight flew in to Chicago, then to Stockholm and finally I arrived at my destination, Tallinn. In my 9 year career of playing professional basketball, my time in Estonia, was the only time I had a serious bout with ill health. When I boarded my departing flight from Detroit to Chicago, I had a pounding headache that would not allow me to sleep on the 45 minute flight. After arriving in Chicago, the pain worsened and I quickly checked my luggage at the Scandinavian Airlines counter then requested wheel chair assistance to get to my designated departure gate.

By this time, I was really in bad shape. So I decided to lie on the floor by my departure gate using my coat as a pillow. The two hours that I waited at the gate seemed like two days. My body was so weak, that I could not muster up the strength to turn off my lap top, nor could I have fended off anyone who may have desired to rob me of it.

I would wake up for 1 minute and pass out for another 20 minutes and that went on until my flight departed Chicago. Upon arriving in Stockholm, it seemed as though my body had taken a serious plunge for the worst and I needed to be helped off the plane and through the Swedish Customs. Their airport staff did a streamlined job of helping me find my passport and travel documents, because I was absolutely out of it. They rolled me in a wheelchair to the departure gates for Tallinn, Estonia. At this point, I just wanted to get to Estonia and get to a bed or a hospital. Thankfully, the flight was only about an hour more.

We finally arrived in Tallinn at about 11 o'clock at night. The best part about this trip was that I was going to get a chance to play for Coach Chaz Sacks, who had coached me before. I had known Coach Sacks for quite a while, as our paths had crossed each others' in the basketball circuit. When Coach sacks arrived to pick me up, I could not have been any happier. The coach insisted that I stay with him the first few days of my stay because I was noticeably too weak for any activities. Every player has their own apartment which is covered by the team but I could not be left alone with my physical condition.

Chaz had to call the Talinn EMS (Emergency Medical Services) who picked me up and rushed me to the hospital. I was admitted and after the hospital performed several tests, it was discovered I had pneumonia. Additionally, I had "blown an ear drum on the plane," which was the cause of my non-stop headaches. The doctor prescribed medication and informed me that I would be unable to play or do anything for 2 months. He ordered me to stay in bed. I knew the massive power of pneumonia as my grandmother, uncle, and others I know have died from this illness.

I have strong faith in God so I stayed in prayer and I believed that I would come out healed and back to normal in due time. That is exactly what happened.

Upon being released from the hospital, the doctor told me that "pneumonia is contagious." And to, "Stay out of contact with people and keep your body warm and wrapped up." I was around Chaz for quite a bit, because I lived with him, but I could not help but to think that maybe he would catch pneumonia from being around me. One day I saw Chaz take a small bottle of some "strange substance" and put two drops of it in the green tea (with lemons inside) that he was drinking. He could see me staring at him with the peculiar look on my face, so he said, "I know you want to know why I am doing this. There is a perfectly good reason that I can live with you in this house and not catch pneumonia and, it's called Oil Of Oregano, in fact here try some."

He poured me a glass of water, put in two drops in, and insisted that I drink it. I was not eager to try it but, I was willing, considering my poor health. Coach Sacks had confessed to me that this was his secret to good health which had been a remedy in his family for years. Sacks explained that as a professional coach, or basketball player, who travels frequently and is away from his native country the majority of each year, it is imperative to keep a self preservation kit with you at all times. He continued on by saying "you would not like to be under the care of some foreign doctor who may not be accustomed to providing the standard of health care that you may be accustomed to in the states."

Coach had given me some information that had been missing from my life for many years. After about two weeks of taking the Oil of Oregano, I started to feel like "the old me" again. I thought it to be quite ironic, considering the fact that the doctors had told me that I needed 2 months (they were probably playing it safe because it was really cold there).

I am not saying that Oregano Oil cured me of anything or that I miraculously got up and ran outside to jump into the "Gulf of Finland". However, I am saying that I felt good enough to leave the house and do the everyday things that ordinary people love to do, in fact I was also able to do a few exercises. As you know, most people "must see it to believe it," so I decided to pull out my Sherlock Holmes hat and do some research about this oregano oil.

Ancient 20's teaching points on OREGANO OIL:

- Destroys organisms that contribute to skin infections and digestive problems

- Strengthens the Immune System

- Enhances joint and muscle flexibility

- Promotes great respiratory health

- Fights bronchitis, pneumonia, sore throats, diarrhea, nervous tension, toothache, coughs, skin conditions (i.e. psoriasis and eczema), treats athletes' foot, and indigestion

- Protects you while you are traveling through the world from serious infection

- Eliminate headaches, arthritis, muscle aches or injury

Ideally, you should use one to two drops of oregano oil under your tongue each day. Many people find it easier to just put the drops in their juice or water. According to Dr. Cass Ingram, author of *The Cure is in the Cupboard*, "Wild oregano is a veritable natural mineral treasure-house, containing a density of minerals that would rival, virtually any food".

Dr. Ingram also mentioned that, if you used Oil of Oregano with foods such as meat, eggs, milk, or salad, you will greatly halt the growth of microbes and, thus, reduce the risk of food poisoning. Oregano does something magical in that its' antiseptic abilities inhibits growth of a majority bacteria. This is something that most prescription antibiotics fail to achieve. Keep in mind that while Oregano Oil is a remarkable home remedy, please be advised that:

• Oregano Oil may reduce the body's ability to absorb iron. Therefore, it is recommended that if you are taking this oil daily, you should certainly combine its' use with a regular consumption of iron supplements. This is why it is not wise for pregnant women to use Oregano Oil on a regularly basis

• If you have allergies, you may be sensitive to Oregano Oil

The remedies outlined above are based on, the use of "REAL" Oil Of Oregano. Be sure to read the label before buying. I often cook with oregano leaves so I get a change of pace from consuming the actual oil drops that come in a bottle.

Law Thirteen

SAY NO TO PROCESSED FOODS: "AUSTRIA"

"He who does not mind his belly, will not hardly mind anything else." ~Samuel Johnson

It was time to jump for joy in the town of Klagenfurt, Austria. The citizens and fans had a reason to celebrate because we qualified for the last position for the play-offs. I can remember being relieved of accomplishing that feat as if it were yesterday. The custom of the regular season was to play one game per week. For the final three weeks of the season, we were repeatedly reminded every day, by the coach and team general manager, that these were all MUST WIN games! The idea of losing never entered my mind. But the tension was so high, that one couldn't help but wonder what would happen in the event of a lost game. If I had to choose one thing that I did not like about playing professional basketball outside of America, it would be the fact that, sometimes losing a game could result in the team threatening not to pay the player's salary for that particular month, or they would be extremely late with the payment, to encourage you to play hard and win for the next game. There has only been one time in my career that I had to leave a situation without getting a salary that was owed to me, so I am considered lucky. Needless to say, I enjoyed my time with the Austrians and they were very honorable people, they were people of their word. The best part of Klagenfurt was where I lived. I lived directly in front of one of the most famous lakes in all of Europe. Lake Worthesee. During the winter people from all parts of

Austria and Germany would come to ice-skate on the lake. I had only seen people ice-skate in movies and in Olympic competitions, so this was sort of a surreal situation, especially with the fact that I was literally residing 50 feet from the lake. It was indeed a very peaceful location, so that really helped to take the load off from the rigors of my job. As a point guard in basketball, my job is to make sure that every other man is doing his job on the court and be the leader of the team. That job is often not easy when you are dealing with the egos of grown men who only think of themselves. Having a nice and serene living arrangement to escape to after frustrating days with my teammates really came in handy for me during my time in Austria.

One day, immediately following a hard practice I decided to go home, shower, eat some food and lay down for a while. After about 5 minutes of rest I got up to use the restroom. However, after approximately 20 minutes later I felt the urge to urinate again but this time there was less urine but more of a need to urinate. I thought nothing of it until I made 10 more trips to the restroom within 6 hours! At this point there were so many things that went through my mind like; did I have a kidney stone? Did I have cancer, urinary tract infection or was this something about which I had never heard. I had such a sleepless night! I got up the next day, went to the doctor to take every test I that I possibly could take. Each of the test yielded negative results which was a relief but at the same time it concerned me. How could I urinate and five minutes later, rush to the bathroom to use it again with the feeling of a full bladder? Was it really normal to wake up from my sleep 4 times throughout the night just to use the bathroom? This was indeed puzzling, not to mention the fact that I was a 26 year old professional athlete and in good shape. The timing was pretty impeccable, because I was to head back home to the United States, shortly and thereafter, I could surely get a medical answer and be free of all the mental strife.

Unfortunately, the answers that I sought from my personalphysicians back home were more elusive than a snake in the amazon jungle.

Immediately upon my arrival home in Detroit, I sought out one of the best Urologist in the area. The earliest I could get an appointment was in seven days, so I settled on that. During my visit with the urologist he informed me that I would need a "cystoscopy". What!? A cystoscopy is defined as, a test that allows your doctor to look in the interior lining of the bladder and urethra. It is done by sticking a tube through the tip of the penis/vagina and down through the bladder with a camera. I reluctantly agreed to do the procedure because I knew that it would be pain beyond measure! After several urine test and a cystoscopy Doctor Keller alerted me that I had what was known as "Overactive Bladder". What was this overactive bladder? Besides, I'm not 75 years old, so I should not have any bladder issues in at all. He could not tell me exactly how I had contracted this illness and but the only thing he could say was that "it could be your diet."

According to the *Mayo Clinic*, Overactive bladder can be defined as, a problem with bladder storage function that causes a sudden urge to urinate. The urge may be difficult to suppress, and overactive bladder can lead to the involuntary loss of urine (incontinence).

He prescribed for me a drug that is very common for people who suffer from overactive bladder and interstitial cystitis. Getting a prescription baffled me, because I thought that a doctor's job was to cure the patient and explain how to avoid any future illnesses. I later discovered that "technically speaking," a health care practitioner does not have to cure you. Even if there is a cure available, they only have to treat you! During this time I really started to develop major suspicions about the health care industry. Once I left the doctor's office, I began to research everything

I could about this illness. I was determined to get healthy.

I eventually found some information that would help me greatly with the illness and it did not come from any prescriptions or over the counter drugs from a store. In my quest to find out more about this illness, I consulted a nutritionist. The first question that she posed to me was, "Do you eat a lot of processed foods?" I did not really have an answer for her because I did not know what processed foods entailed. She said "Do you like frozen dinners, canned foods, cookies, or lunch meat?" I replied, "Of course I do. Doesn't everyone?" She chuckled quietly, as if I was a foolish child who had no direction. She informed me that this was more likely, than not, the reason for the overactive bladder.

I reflected back, on all of the food that I had eaten while in Austria and it corresponded with what she had said. I ate frozen fish sticks almost every day. I had my family send me a "care package" with crackers and pecan shortbread cookies. I had self inflected an illness without my knowledge. I would have sworn that I was eating "half way healthy," but it was not so. What was inside these processed foods that made them so unhealthy?

By definition, *processed food* is any food that you can buy in a can, jar, packet or bottle. Processed foods have been altered from their natural state for safety reasons, as well as convenience. Most methods used for processing foods include canning, freezing, refrigeration, dehydration and aseptic processing.

Ancient 20's three major issues with processed foods:

* *They contain food additives.* They are added to processed foods to enhance their shelf life and make them last longer. Salt, sugar and vinegar were some of the first additives to be used in food preservation. With the advent of processed foods, there has been a huge explosion in the chemical

adulteration of foods with additives, which is more of a serious issue.

- *The healthy stuff is removed.* When you process foods you tend to lose a lot of the nutrients and fibers thus making the purpose of processing redundant. Vitamins and minerals are destroyed because the intensity of heat used in the processing.

- *There is almost nothing left.* When manufacturers add some of the lost and destroyed vitamins and minerals, they say the product is "fortified with vitamins and minerals," to make it sound more appealing. The truth is, very little of what is lost can be put back in, so do not fall for this marketing trick.

Ancient 20's additives to beware of, when you shop and read labels for foods that you consume:

- Aspartame – Sweetener

- Preservatives

- Chemical – Antidexoidants

- Artificial Colors

- MSG

- Nitrates/Nitrites

- Parabons

- Sulfites

It is estimated that we consume about 5 kilograms (approximately 11 pounds) of food additives as preservatives, colors, bleaches, flavors, emulsifiers and stabilizers in the food that we consume each year. This not only results in extra work for our body to remove them, but frequently trigger asthma attacks; rashes; respiratory disturbances; hyperactivity in children, and in some people, an abnormal sensitivity to prescribed medications, particularly aspirin.

Nutritionist *Shereen Jegtvig* is co-author of "Superfoods For Dummies" and also believes that processed foods are not the choice for those who desire optimum health. Jegtvig states that "Many processed foods are made with trans fats, saturated fats, and large amounts of sodium and sugar."

Below is a list from Dr. Jegtvig of some the processed foods that may not be as healthy as fresh foods:

- Canned foods with lots of sodium.

- White breads and pastas made with refined white flour, which are not as healthy as those made with whole grains (Depending if the person has Celiac Disease or not).

- Packaged high calorie snack foods, like chips and cheese snacks.

- High-fat convenience foods, like cans of ravioli.

- Frozen fish stick dinners and frozen dinners.

- Packaged cakes and cookies.

- Boxed meal mixes.

- Sugary breakfast cereals plus snacks.

- Processed meats. This is very important because the nitrates and nitrites in these meats may increase your risk of colorectal, kidney and stomach cancer. Processed meats include hot dogs, bologna, sausage, ham and other packaged lunch meats.

On the contrary, not all processed foods are unhealthy. There is one special type of foods that can be processed and those are "frozen vegetables". Although fresh may be best, freezing vegetables preserves vitamins and minerals which makes them convenient to cook and eat all year around.

Remember if you are going to choose lunch meat, buy from the fresh deli in your local supermarket. If you wish to have a steak, go to your local butcher at your supermarket. In the end, the fresh way is the best way. I had to fall ill before I caught on but luckily I recovered, maybe the next person might not be as lucky. There is an old saying that states; "A wise man will learn from the mistakes of others, but a fool will learn from his own mistakes." Why not take the path of the wise man and learn from my challenges.

Law Fourteen

LEAN MORE TOWARDS POULTRY AND FISH: "TAHITI**"**

"Pork, in every form is indigestible and should never be eaten by persons of weak digestion, by young children, nor by the old and feeble." ~The Picayune's Creole Cook Book

The year of 1998 was a great year for me, athletically speaking. I had just completed my sophomore year in college. I was playing the best basketball of my life up until that point. As a result of my play, I had been chosen to be a counselor at the prestigious Michael Jordan's basketball camp. Some of the best collegiate players in America were invited as counselors for the younger kids. On occasion the counselors would play pickup games at night. This was a great way for me to gauge my abilities against those players from "big time" college programs such as Duke University, Wake Forest University, University of Michigan and other prestigious universities. Many of the counselors from the camp went on to become NBA players, so it was a great experience for me. One day the counselors were allowed to play against each other in front of the entire camp staff and the campers. Michael Jordan was in attendance and watched the entire game that particular day. I felt that I played a pretty good game and my confidence was growing each day as I played against the elite players from around the country. Directly, after this particular game, Michael Jordan himself approached me and began talking to me about what he saw in my ability.

He approached me and said, "You played a great game but you have to work more on your right hand. I could detect that you are left hand dominant and your right hand is weaker. So, you have to work on that weakness if you are to become a great player at the next level." He then shook my hand as he walked away being swarmed by the media who were covering the camp.

Just when I thought that I had reached the pinnacle of my summer, I received a call from my university's assistant coach, David Glassman. Coach "Glass", as the players affectionately nicknamed him, called to ask me if I wanted to be part of a team from the United States that was to travel to the country of Tahiti to compete in an international friendly tournament with teams from France and Tahiti. I gladly accepted the opportunity and within one month, I departed Chicago on a flight going to Papeete, Tahiti (via Los Angeles, California). The only thing that I knew about Tahiti was that it was famous for vacations and that it was located somewhere in the heart of the South Pacific Ocean. With so little information, I had no expectations. But my goal was to learn as much as I could and represent the United States in a manner reflecting excellence.

Being that Tahiti is a part of the French Polynesia, most of its inhabitants spoke French. All at once my lack of paying attention to my 11th and 12th grade French class teachers came back to bite. OUCH! Until that day, Tahiti, was the only place in the world that I have traveled been that had black sand beaches. I kept thinking, "How on earth could there be black sand on a beach?" It is still a mystery that I will have to look into deeper over time. I attributed it to one of God's many miracle creations. On a side note, I have also never seen a place where CRABS walked the streets! When you are in a remote place such as Papeete, you have to be very selective with what you eat. The best thing about living on an island is the fact that you have an unlimited supply of fresh fish. While I was on the island I had seen the Tahitian's eat all kinds of meat, but many of them lived on fish and chicken.

I eat beef to get certain proteins but I do not eat it often. Beef is loaded with great nutrients, but it can also tax the body in the digestive system. In the beginning we were playing it safe and eating a lot of scrambled eggs to get our protein intake since we did not know much about where to get our food.

After a few days we became somewhat acclimated to the way of life. I ate fish or chicken before each game, while in Tahiti. I was very happy with how I felt during and after the games. In the United States, I used to eat steak and potatoes for my pre-game meal and I could not understand why I felt so heavy during the game. Even during high school when I ate pork, my body never felt quite the same, as when I ate chicken, fish or turkey. When I was younger, I felt as though I had a high metabolism, so I didn't think that what I ate mattered that much. But, there was one particular day that stands out in my mind. We had been given the day free, which meant we did not have to practice or play a game. This particular day was a day I chose to take my scooter (we all rented scooters for the entire time there) and ride around Papeete to check out the island. I got a little hungry about 30 minutes into my navigation, so I decided to grab something quickly from one of the road side vendors. The vendor was selling "chicken kabob," and some unfamiliar fish. I'm sure you know which one I chose!

The vendor must have been used to the tourists, as he started a small conversation with me about my trip to Tahiti (and he also wanted money). Waiting for my kabob to finish cooking, I asked the gentleman where the beef steak was.

He replied in an angry tone, "too much beef no good for you," while waving his index finger in a condemning manner. He then pointed at the chicken kabob that he was preparing, made a muscle with his arm and said, "poulet et poissons make me a strong old man". He was in good shape for a man of 71 years of age. *Poulet et poisons* means "chicken and fish" in the French language. He carried on about too much beef being very difficult for the digestive system to break down and how most people would do their bodies a favor by incorporating the "fish and chicken diet" into their daily lives. When I mentioned pork to him he turned his back on me and started laughing and pointing to the sky saying, "God no like pig". I was actually amused to hear some of his ideologies and from where they came. As a person who reads the Bible, I was aware of the Old Testament scriptures and God's dislike for pork.

In the Islamic society, pork is not permitted, as is in the Hebrew-Israelite, or Jewish religions. *Dr. E.A. Widner,* in his article *"Pork, Man and Disease"* states:

"Pork although one of the most common articles of diet, is one of the most injurious. God did not prohibit the Hebrews from eating swine's' flesh merely to show his authority, but because it was not a proper article of food for man".

I do not wish to turn this chapter into any form of religious discussion. But I would like to bring up the fact that ninety-nine percent of all followers, or practitioners of the Bible whom I have come in contact with, love to debate about pork and the dietary law. Their claim is that the Book of Leviticus is not valid when it comes to the enforcing of the dietary law, because it is a part of the Old Testament.

People also argue that in the New Testament Jesus comes and wipes the Old Testament laws away. Based on a chapter in the book of Matthew, it can be debated that the Old Testament does carry some weight in Jesus' eyes. Let's take a closer look at *Matthew, chapter 5: verses 17-19* and see what Jesus says:

"Think not that I am come to destroy the law, or the prophets(the old testament): I am not come to destroy, but to fulfill. For verily I say unto you, Till heaven and earth pass, one jot or one tittle shall in no wise pass from the law, till all be fulfilled. Whosoever therefore shall break one of these least commandments, and shall teach men so, he shall be called the least in the kingdom of heaven: but whosoever shall do and teach them, the same shall be called great in the kingdom of heaven". You are certainly allowed to form your own opinions based upon your faith.

Based on the article from *BBC News* in 2005 called, *"Red meat linked to cancer risk,"* eating very well done cooked red meat may:

"Increase the likelihood of cancer because carcinogenic compounds called heterocyclic amines are created during the cooking process. Heterocyclic amines may not explain why red meat is more harmful than other meat, however, as these compounds are also found in poultry and fish, which have not been linked to an increased cancer risk".

Health officials say that regular consumption of red meat without vitamin and mineral supplementation has also been linked to bone loss, type 2 diabetes, hypertension and arthritis. I am not sure how true this statement is, because it has been known for more than 25 years that, the lack of specific trace minerals are the underlying reasons for these illnesses. It is most important to remember that the manner with which you cook your meat has a huge affect on your body.

According to Dr. Joel Wallach, author of *Hell's Kitchen*, people should not burn their meats when they cook. Burnt animal fats present many problems for your body. The consumption of burnt meat will surely bring about illnesses to your body because they aid unhealthy free radicals and make your digestive system work very hard to break down your food. Poaching, boiling, broiling and baking are the only healthy ways to cook your meats.

For reasons such as the ones mentioned above, fish is always a great option, for those who want a healthy meal that is easy to prepare.

Ancient 20's facts on eating fish:

- Fish "can provide an excellent source of Omega-3 fatty acids, vitamins and minerals that benefit general health," says *Maxine Hayes*, of the Washington State Health Department. Omega-3 decreases heart disease, reduces blood pressure, helps prevent abnormal heart rhythms and promotes healthy brain function.

- The American Heart Association recommends at least two servings of fish per week to help prevent heart disease, lower blood pressure and reduce the risks of heart attacks and strokes.

- The American Diabetes Association feels that fish is a great choice for people with diabetes. The high protein supply aids in the regulation of blood sugar. Fish is a good low calorie, high protein choice to assist in weight loss.

- If you bake, poach, broil or grill, the cook time for fish is ten minutes, for every inch of thickness. If it is frozen, then it's twenty minutes for every inch.

- Rush Institute for Healthy Aging states, "People who eat at least one meal of fish per week will be significantly less likely to develop Alzheimer's disease, than those who never eat fish.

- Fish is low fat and is a good quality protein filled with riboflavin (Vitamin B-2) and Vitamin D, which aids in calcium absorption. Fish is also rich in calcium and phosphorous and includes potassium, a mineral needed for muscles, nerves, and fluid balance in the body, iodine and magnesium.

When I was younger, I only ate chicken, because of its' taste. I did not know what benefits it held. *World's Healthiest Foods* says that chicken "Is *the world's primary source of animal protein and healthy alternative to red meat"*. Even better news is that chicken is very versatile, in that you can cook it anyway that you desire, or add it to many foods to accentuate its flavor.

Ancient 20's facts on Chicken:

- Provides 67.6% of the daily value for protein in 4 ounces

- Protects against age related cognitive decline

- Contains B vitamins (pyridoxine, niacin) for energy

- Contains protein that protects against bone loss in elder people

- Skinless chicken is one of the lowest-fat meats available

Holidays such as Easter, Thanksgiving, and Independence Day give little "wiggle room" for healthy eating habits. But,take into consideration exactly what the outcome will be for your health and heavily examine the meats that go in to your body. It is your duty to give your body the highest quality of service that it deserves, because in the end, it will only produce the results that correspond to the care it is given.

Law Fifteen

DRINK JUICE FROM FRESH FRUITS & VEGETABLES:
"DOMINICAN REPUBLIC"

"Shall I not have intelligence with the earth? Am I not partly leaves and vegetable mould myself." ~Henry David Thoreau

My second favorite country in the world is the Dominican Republic. The median salary for all workers in the Dominican Republic rounds off at about 10,000 Dominican pesos (roughly $300 dollars) per month. I have never been to a country where the inhabitants work so hard, for such a small pay. Dominican Republic is located in the Caribbean on the same island as Haiti. Because of its' tropical climate, the Dominican Republic boasts an agricultural system that is second to none. They grow and harvest all their foods, so there is not a need to search elsewhere for nourishment. In fact, their natural resources are so rich in fruits and vegetables that they are engaged in plenty of commercial trade with the United States and Cuba. You may not find a better agricultural engineer in the world than in the DR. The farmers spend long hours tilling the land to be sure that everything turns out perfectly. The reason for their expertise is simple. Their lives depend upon it. Due to the country's political infrastructure, job security is not certain. If you are under a certain political party (PRD or PLD) and a new president elect is voted in after 4 years, then you can be sure that you will be left without a job when the newly elected president does enter into office if you are not apart of his political party. Most job situations in the DR are obtained through political circles or ties. The Dominicans may refer to it as "un anillo". This means, a ring of people who help each other. This is why being a great farmer is a much more stable occupation.

The name of the city in which I lived at the time was called Puerto Plata. According to historians, Puerto Plata was the first city discovered in New World (before he discovered the United States) and the Dominican Republic by the great Christopher Columbus. The translation for Puerto Plata, means "Silver Door". Puerto Plata is a city known primarily for tourism and its love of sports. I had the honor of playing in their professional basketball league in which my team had won the championship. Because of the flaming temperatures, I always needed something to drink before, during and after the practice. Outside of the practice site always stood an elderly man who sold "jugo" (means juice in English). For 20 to 25 pesos (about 70 cents) you could get a nice sized cup of fresh juice made right in front of you within one minute. Sometimes his cart would be full of oranges, tamarinds, grapefruits, and lemons so I was in juice heaven, so to speak. I had never heard of the juice "tamarindo" (or tamarind) which was a fruit that was famous in the Caribbean, Central, and South America. After the first cup of tamarindo I was blown away! I had never had fresh juice made right in front of me. Secondly, that I had never drunk juice from a fruit that I had never seen or heard of and it tasted great. I was spending about 100 pesos per day ($3) on juices alone. I drank passion fruit, papaya, and other local juices that were even better than the tamarindo juice.

It was quite a transition coming, from drinking, supposed "drinks with electrolytes", back in the United States, to consuming natural juices that gave me so much more energy. There was not a day that went by that I did not drink some kind of juice. If I thought I was impressed with the juices then I do not have a word to tell you how I felt about the food. I was fortunate in that I have family who live in the Dominican Republic. I grew up in the United States, so I was not used to their customs, but I could speak the language (Spanish). The cornerstone food for the Dominicans is known as the "plantain". You may have seen this vegetable in the store and mistaken it for a huge banana that was not ripe. The plantain is in the banana family but it is not exactly a banana. It is normally prepared by being boiled or fried. I used to eat so many before a game that I would have to arrive at the gym about 2 hours before the game to try to sweat as much as I could to cut some weight. The plantains are that good.

The issue here is that many Americans prefer to consume their juice in the form of artificial and carbonated drinks. These drinks contain a ridiculous amount of acid, fructose and concentrated sugars. What is worse is that those same people love to drink soda with their meals. Harvard Medical School's Dr. Jennifer Daniels states, "Fruit juice, when put in a bottle, is heated up and loses all nutritional value. The enzymes die, so it is of no use."

As a conscious health being, I can honestly say that I would not allow my worst enemy to drink soda because it has absolutely NO health benefits. The main reason you should avoid drinking carbonated drinks is that they neutralize the "good stomach acid". Stomach acid plays a vital role in the body, in that it is needed to help absorb nutrients and break down foods. If you neutralize the acid then your stomach has a harder time digesting the food, which allows the food to sit longer in your stomach and ferment. If it is done on a consistent basis, those foods may begin to cause one or a host of nutritional deficiency diseases. In order for a person to be as healthy as can be, they need to eat and drink as NATURAL and RAW as they can. You do not have to buy juice, per se, if you consume a certain amount of fruits and vegetables daily. How you consume your fruits will be CRITICAL to your entire health.

In his famous article titled *Eating Fruits* Dr. Stephen Mak says, "Fruits should be eaten on an empty stomach." He goes on to say that, if you eat fruit fruit on an empty stomach it will play a major role to detoxify your system, supplying you with a great deal of energy for weight loss and other life activities.

Mak goes on to show us an example of why fruits should not be eaten after a meal. The example states, "Let's say you eat two slices of bread and then a slice of fruit. The slice of fruit is ready to go straight through the stomach into the intestines, but it is prevented from doing so. In the meantime the whole meal rots and ferments and turns into acid. The minute the fruit comes in contact with the food in the stomach and digestive juices, the entire mass of food begins to spoil." I like to eat mine before each meal or if I am on the go I will use my blender to make a shake (smoothie) with fruits and vegetables.

New York Times Best Selling Author and the world's foremost expert on juicing, Jay Kordich, has a very unique view of why you should juice your fruits. The juicing king, was diagnosed with bladder cancer at the age of 25 and after he had exhausted all options, he decided to go on a fresh raw juices diet. He has been cured of his cancer until this day and he is now 89 years of age. Kordich states, "The reason for juicing is to separate the juice from the fiber, so that when you drink pulp free juice, you will have 100% of the food value in your bloodstream, pre-digested, in a short period of time. If you choose to consume the fruits and vegetables normally, then you are asking your body to process the food, which has to pass through many stages."

Late 1800's chemist and nutritionist, *Dr. Henry C. Sherman*, of Columbia University, gives a much bolder statement, on the importance of consuming fresh plant based foods. Sherman states, "To be absolutely healthy and not disease plagued early in life, one needs nutrients to the equivalent of eating 15 pounds of green and yellow vegetables and plant life daily." That is a pretty big statement. This is essentially saying that we must consume a great deal of fruits and veggies to be healthy on a daily basis. Jay Kordich, in his infinite wisdom, understood that no one could possibly eat this many plant based foods on the daily basis, so the best way to consume them would be by juicing the fresh fruits and vegetables.

Dominican people truly live "off of the land" and it is evident in their physical appearances. I have seen plenty of healthy senior citizens.

Growing up in America I find that most people eat the common fruits and vegetables such as: apples, oranges, celery, tomatoes, grapes, lemons, garlic, broccoli, carrots, kiwi, etc.

The 5 vegetables I consistently ate while in the Dominican Republic:

- *Avocado* – Native to Central America this vegetable targets the health and function of the womb and cervix of the female. When a woman eats just one avocado per week, it balances hormones, sheds unwanted birth weight, and prevents cervical cancers. Amazingly, it takes exactly nine months to grow an avocado from blossom to ripened fruit. There are over 14,000 photolytic chemical constituents of nutrition in each one of these foods (modern day science has only studied and named about 141 of them). It also heals skin problems and those that suffer from digestive and circulatory problems. The beautiful hair and skin of the Dominican women can be contributed to this veggie.

- *Sweet Potato* – According to food service industry professional and author *Peggy Trowbridge,"* Sweet potatoes are relatively low in calories and have no fat. They are rich in beta-carotene, having five times the recommended daily allowance of vitamin A in one sweet potato, as well as loaded with potassium. These nutrients help to prevent against heart attack and stroke. The potassium helps maintain fluid and electrolyte balance in the body cells, as well as normal heart function and blood pressure.

- *Eggplant* – Its' fiber content is high, which helps the digestive process and also acts against coronary heart disease. Eggplant not only features a number of vitamins, proteins and minerals but they also contain phytonutrients. These "special nutrients" act as antioxidants. In phytonutrients in the eggplants, there are phenolic compounds, such as caffeic and chlorogenic acid, and flavanoids, like nasunin. Potassium in eggplant brings a balance in salt intake and maintains a nice level of hydration. Eggplant also contain folate, magnesium, niacin, copper, manganese, and thiamine (vitamin – B1).

- *Onion* – Is characterized by its rich content of thiosulfinates, sulfides, sulfoxides, and other odoriferous sulfur compounds. The cysteine sulfoxides are primarily responsible for the onion flavor and produce the eye-irritating compounds that induce lacrimation. So now you know the reason for your tears when you peel an onion. Early American settlers used wild onions to treat colds, coughs, asthma, and to repel insects. In Chinese medicine, onions have been used to treat angina, bacterial infections, and breathing problems.

- *Plantains* – The backbone of the Dominican culture besides beans and rice. Plantains are a part of the "banana family" but cannot be eaten in the same manner as a "normal banana", although they do share similar health benefits. They are an essential food for anyone suffering from

Seasonal Affective Depression (SAD) because they contain natural mood enhancers. Plantains have been dubbed by the East Indians as "natures' secret of perpetual youth". The reason for this claim is that this vegetable helps your body retain more calcium, phosphorous and nitrogen which will help rejuvenate your healthy tissues.

As a person who seeks to learn, I can unashamedly say that I never paid much attention to these vegetables and I have seen them countless numbers of times over the course of my life. When you see 15 vitamin C commercials per day about oranges you tend to believe that oranges from Florida or California are your best chances at nutrition. Or maybe you were in your doctors' office one day and you saw a poster about broccoli and how the carotenoid lutein and folic acid that it contains help fight cancer. When you become programmed on what you should do or eat, you normally don't think about any other possibilities that exist because, in your mind there are no other possibilities. That is the very purpose of television and commercials.

I wish to convey an example to you of this "programming" through examples that I recall from "Old Country Western Movies". One might ask, what does this have to do with this chapter? Allow me to show you. Many times in the old country western movies before the shooting or killing of a cowboy, the shooter would ask if the cowboy had "one last request" and most times the cowboy would reply "give me a cigarette". Ask yourself, "Is a cigarette really more important than seeing your loved ones or kissing your children goodbye?" Certainly it is not! However, you are lead to believe that a cigarette is so invigorating that a man would request one as his last dying wish. In turn, people subconsciously begin to believe what they see and thus the sales of cigarettes skyrockets around the country. These are known as subliminal messages. It may sound silly but it is very true.

Here are some of the fruits that regenerated my body during and after practices while in the Dominican Republic:

- *Grapefruit* – Very helpful in removing or dissolving inorganic calcium which may have formed in the cartilage of the joint as in arthritis, as a result of an excessive consumption of devitalized white flour products. Fresh grapefruit contains organic salicylic acid which aids in dissolving such inorganic calcium in the body. It is rich in lycopene (the red color/pigment); it helps to prevent the occurrence of a tumor and cancer. Lastly, it can help in weight loss since it is low in sodium and high in fat burning enzymes. Low sodium intake can help flush out excess water that is caused by high sodium food.

- *Passion fruit* – One of the many nutritional benefits of passion fruit is that their seed (one cup) contains almost 25 grams of fiber. Fiber attaches itself to the buildup found in the colon wall, pulls it out and makes the colon clean and clear from disturbances. A similar process takes place in the valves of the heart whereby fiber flushes out the buildup of fat and cholesterol in the heart, protecting the body against heart attacks, heart disease and strokes.

- *Papaya* – The unique protein-digesting enzymes; papain and chymopapain have been shown to help lower inflammation and to improve healing from burns in addition to helping digestion of proteins. The antioxidant nutrients found in papaya, including vitamin C, vitamin E and beta-carotene, are also very good at reducing inflammation. Case studies indicate that this food taken alone for two to three days has a highly beneficial tonic effect upon the stomach and intestines. The juice of the papaya aids in relieving infections of the colon and has a tendency to break down pus and mucus reached by the juice.

- *Tamarind* – The pulp, leaves, and flowers in various combinations are applied on painful and swollen joints. The heated juice is used to cure conjunctivitis. Eye drops made from tamarind seeds may be a treatment for dry eye syndrome. Tamarind seed "polysaccharide" is adhesive, enabling it to stick to the surface of the eye longer than other eye preparations. This fruit is also used to treat bile disorders, acts as a laxative, promotes a healthy heart and is gargled to treat sore throat.

- *Strawberry* – Highly rated as a skin cleansing food, even though the skin eruptions may appear at first in some cases. Cleans the blood of harmful toxins. There have been reports that strawberries helped cases of syphilis. When cut in half and rubbed on the teeth and gums it removes tartar from the teeth and strengthens and heals the gums. The juice should be allowed to remain on the teeth as long as possible in order to dissolve the tartar. The mouth may then be rinsed with warm water. Data reported in a study published in the *Archives of Ophthalmology* indicates that "eating 3 or more servings of fruit per day may lower your risk of age-related macular degeneration (ARMD), the primary cause of vision loss in older adults, by 36%, compared to persons who consume less than 1.5 servings of fruit daily". Strawberries played a big role in the study because of its vitamins and carotenoids.

Do not feel that you need to be on an island to have access to these fruits and many other fruits that are not so common. As you research, you will see that the city in which you live or a surrounding city will more than likely have fruit stores that sell fruits from all over the world. So, get to your local fruit market today and try something new.

Law Sixteen

TRY NATURAL HERBS AND SPICES FOR FOOD SEASONINGS: "UNITED STATES OF AMERICA"

"Once you get a spice in your home, you have it forever. Women never throw out spices. The Egyptians were buried with their spices. I know which one I'm taking when I go."
~Erma Bombeck

One of my most life-altering years happened back in 1990-1991. I was 12 years old at the time, so I was a bit mischievous and not doing so great in school. During the summer of 1990, I was sent to live a year with my grandparents in Greenwood, Mississippi. As you enter Greenwood, there is a sign that says "Welcome to Greenwood, the *cotton capital* of the world." I did not think about what I had read on the sign at that moment, but it did register that my life was going to be a bit different coming from the urban streets of Detroit, Michigan to the Mississippi Delta.

There are 3 things that I will never forget about that year, while in Mississippi. First, I grew an amazing 6 inches in one year, which took me from 5 ft7 inches to 6 ft 1 inch in a years' time. I think it was because of the vegetation! Secondly, I took a 15 pound barbell that my father had given me before I left Detroit and exercised with it 3 to 4 times per week. I consistently did 100 bicep curls and 100 behind the neck push presses 3 to 4 times per week, so I got incredibly strong for a kid my age. Lastly, my grandmother would make almost all of our meals from scratch and she always had a knack for creating things in the kitchen. My mom was a great cook as well, but I have to say that my grandmother was the "master cook" of the family. She was very big on using herbs and spices for adding flavor to the food. In the southern part of the United States, most meals consisted of pork, which meant that the meals did not need any extra "iodized salt" because pork in itself contained a high salt content.

I can remember my grandmother making plum jelly from scratch and storing it in the pantry for months. She would give it away or I would claim a good portion of it with those homemade biscuits that she prepared. At the age of 12 you are not worried what ingredients your grandmother uses to cream or fry corn, because your only concern is that it tastes great. Through all of my folly, I did manage to have memorable moments in the kitchen with grandma. My favorite days were the days when she made "homemade French fries." During my time living in my parent's house, I had only seen them cook fries with salt, pepper, and seasoned salt. I was fine with that because they tasted great.

Since I was the youngest person in the house I was also the grunt. A grunt is defined as "A common or unskilled worker; laborer." This meant that I was the low man on the totem pole. So, I had to do all of the tedious chores that no one else would do, including peeling potatoes. After I would slice the potatoes, my grandmother cut up an onion in the potatoes and sprinkled a blend of herbs on top. I later learned that it was called, Mrs. Dash. I asked her why did she not use salt and pepper like my mom and dad and she replied "Because herbs and spices are good for you and you need to try something new anyway." Being a kid, I knew nothing about "blood pressure" but I can remember people making a big deal about eating too much salt because it was said by doctors that salt makes your blood pressure rise.

Dr. Joel Wallach, author of *Black Gene Lies*, informs us that salt does NOT cause high blood pressure. Salt is actually something that the body needs. It is an essential nutrient. The way to determine if you are eating too much salt is when it tastes salty. When a farmer puts out a salt lick for a cow, he cannot stand there for the entire day to monitor the amount of licks that the cow takes from the salt lick. The cow will stop licking from the salt lick when the taste is no longer pleasant. This method should also be a blueprint for humans.

Needless to say, I ate those fries and they tasted even better than the normally seasoned fries that I had been accustomed to eating.

The majority of the people whom I have encountered, have always felt that healthy foods taste nasty and the unhealthy foods taste great. That was my belief, before I ate those fried potatoes that my grandmother had cooked. Afterward, my perception had changed for the better. She also went on to tell me that I should learn how to incorporate spices and herbs and even some vegetables as primary flavoring instruments instead of salt. Too much salt can cause many ailments for which we may not be aware. Acne, headaches, fatigue and thirst (because it may induce such a sensation by depleting moisture in the mucous membranes of the mouth and throat) are all examples of known sicknesses from too much salt intake.

Senior medical writer for WebMD, *Daniel J. DeNoon,* wrote an article on salt that stated:

"New data shows that the average U.S. adult consumes one-and-a-half teaspoons of salt every day. That's a half teaspoon more than the basic daily recommendation of one teaspoon (about 2,300 milligrams of sodium). But the recommendation is much lower for people with "high blood

pressure", people over 40, and all African-American adults. These groups should be eating no more than two-thirds of a teaspoon of salt (about 1,500 milligrams of sodium) per day. More than two out of three Americans – some 145.5 million of us – are in those categories, the CDC" (Center of Disease Control and Prevention).

The **American Dietic Association** suggests that instead of adding salt to flavor food, use spices. Try replacing salt with the following spices in your next meal:

- Nutmeg: potato, chicken, fish, cauliflower, broccoli, cabbage dishes

- Rosemary: chicken, fish, sauces, stuffing, potatoes, peas, lima beans

- Sesame: salads, breads, chicken, vegetables

- Allspice: stew, tomatoes, gravy

- Basil: fish, lamb, salads, soups and sauces

- Cayenne Pepper: soups, casserole, barbequed poultry and lean meats

- Cinnamon: sweet potato, squash, breads

- Curry: meat, chicken and fish dishes, tomatoes, sauces and rice

- Dill: fish, chicken, vegetables, potatoes, salads and pasta

- Garlic: pasta dishes, poultry, fish, salads, soups, lean meats

- Lemon or Lime Juice: fish, poultry, salads, vegetables, sauces

- Mint: salads, potatoes, bulgur, beans

Ancient 20's three favorite spices and their medicinal benefits:

• *Cinnamon* – One of the first human studies was published in 2003 in a medical journal called *Diabetes Care*. Sixty people with type 2 diabetes took 1.3, or 6 grams of cinnamon in pill form daily, an amount roughly equivalent to one quarter of a teaspoon to 1 teaspoon of cinnamon. After 40 days, all 3 amounts of cinnamon reduced fasting blood glucose by 18 to 29%, triglycerides by 23 to 30%, LDL cholesterol by 7 to 27%, and total cholesterol by 12 to 26%. In conclusion, it is safe to say that cinnamon fights diabetes.

• *Garlic* – The potency of garlic has been acknowledged for more than 500 years. In ancient times, garlic was used as a remedy for intestinal disorders, flatulence, worms, respiratory infections, skin diseases, wounds, symptoms of aging, and many other ailments. Through the middle ages into World War II, the use of garlic to treat wounds surfaced repeatedly. It was ground up or sliced and was applied directly to wounds to inhibit the spread of infections.

• *Rosemary* – can be consumed in the forms of tea, tincture, capsules or ethereal oils. Rosemary consumption improves digestion, fights against obesity, liver diseases, gastritis, cholesterolemia, bronchic asthma, edemas, and adjusts fast heart beats caused especially by irritability, coffee or tobacco excess. Because of its antiseptic and tonic properties, rosemary is extremely beneficial in cases of fainting, influenza, hangovers, asthma, bronchitis, cramps, constipation, cystitis, headaches, polypus, colds, cough, sinusitis or muscular pains. The plant also has a good influence on the blood circulation and blood pressure.

Being healthy is not something that you can try to achieve once or twice a week. It is a life style choice that you must make for yourself. We are not perfect beings and maybe you will have a day that you slip in your diet regimen. Do not be alarmed, for it is part of the process with overcoming all difficult tasks. My goal through this book is to make natural health a way of life for you.

Law Seventeen

MACA ROOT HERB FOR ENERGY: "SWITZERLAND"

"Failure is more frequently from want of energy than want of capital." ~Daniel Webster

We arrived late to the airport so we did not have time to check our bags. We were instructed to leave our luggage and proceed through the double doors to the jet. We had just won the championship 4 days prior and now we were leaving the former republic of Yugoslavia on a private jet to Lugano, Switzerland. I had always envisioned myself with my own private jet, but I did not imagine that I would be a passenger on a private jet at the age of 25. It was a great feeling to not have to check bags or worry about any travel arrangements as I was accustomed to handling my own travel itinerary. The jet held about 6 people including the pilot, so we were free to move about and do whatever we wished.

There was no one yelling on a microphone "please fasten your seatbelts and turn off all electronic devices", as we were gearing up for departure. During the flight we cruised over 2 countries with the first being Slovenia and the second being Albania. The reason for the trip was because of a promise fulfilled by the team owners, that if we won the championship, they would bring everyone to their luxurious hotel in Switzerland. They were wealthy Albanian businessmen whom had worked their way up through poverty to become owners of an empire that had grossed 700 million Euros in 2004 alone.

We arrived safely in Lugano, Switzerland, which I must say is, until this day, the best vacation place to which I have been. Their hotel's name was the Swiss Diamond Hotel. The Swiss Diamond Hotel is located right on "Lake Lugano", which serves as the divider between Switzerland and Italy. Lugano has been nicknamed "The Monte Carlo of Switzerland" by an ever growing number of celebrities, entertainers and successful athletes. I could swim to Italy in 10 to 15 minutes, that's how close the two countries were.

After we arrived to the hotel, the team owner, Emil, gave the other two American players and me "Carte Blanche" while staying in the hotel. Carte Blanche is a French term for "full powers or blank check". We stayed for ten days! When you are vacationing at a five star hotel in Switzerland, you are bound to run across a few people who own small fortunes. I had dinner with the owner of an airline company, the brother of the prime minister of a Middle Eastern country, and a few other wealthy businessmen. For as much as we are attracted to people whom are wealthy, it is often the person who does not have the wealth that leaves the lasting impression.

One night I had set up a trip to go to Milan, Italy, which was a 45 minutes to an hour drive by car. I had befriended a young Italian man named Danilo, who was working in the bar of the Swiss Diamond Hotel. He had agreed to drive me for "a night on the town" with another player. Danilo had set up a time for us to meet him in the hotel. While waiting in the lobby, I happened to see two beautiful, young, Brazilian women walking with two gentlemen, who looked like they were at least 20 years their senior. One of the gentlemen saw me staring at the women, whom they accompanied. He winked at me and gave me the old "thumbs up" gesture, as if he knew, that I knew, that they were going to have a good ole' time. I watched them walk away with huge smiles on their faces, but in the back of my mind I really wondered how those men could keep up with those young women. I went on to enjoy the night in Milan and thought nothing of the occurrence that I had seen in the lobby.

The next day I woke up just in time for lunch at approximately 11:45 A.M. only to see the same two guys and girls that I had seen in the lobby the night before. I know for a fact that they had arrived back in the hotel after we did but yet they were up the next day before we were. They were eating pool side and the women were in their bikinis feeding fruit to the guys. I started question whether or not I was in a movie. After I finished my meal, I cruised past the swimming pool and the same guy who gave me the thumbs up the night before pulled me to the side and began to speak with me. He had informed me that he and his friend were from Italy but they were vacationing in Lugano with some female friends that they had met in Sao Paolo, Brazil. To my surprise, he spoke great English. He said, "I know what you are thinking", and with a confused look on my face, I replied "Really." He proceeded by saying:

"I have to be in shape to be with young women like this all night long, but I will tell you a secret that I discovered while in Brazil. There is this South American herb called *"Maca Root"* that is totally natural and helps me out a lot. I was taking other sexual performance drugs that were not as healthy, so this is why I use Maca Root now. I am 61 years old, so I have to have an edge. After all I am not young and full of energy like you and your buddies.

A week later I decided to send an email to a Brazilian friend of mine whom I had met during my time in Germany. She confirmed everything that the gentleman had spoke, about with regards to what the *Maca Root* is used. Oddly enough, I was told that Maca Root is being sold all over the world and is easy to buy online. It is not as publicized as other products so that's why many people have not heard about it. At this point I had to take the gentleman's word because the two young Brazilian ladies seemed to be very happy to be with him and his friend. I'm sure his wealth didn't hurt him either. I did my own background check on this maca root to get a third piece of evidence and indeed, I came up with the same positive results. I wondered why I had never heard of this in the United States.

I remembered something that was said to me a long time ago by my neighbor (in the Dominican Republic) when I had an open cut on my foot that would not heal. She told me to rub juice from a Sabila Plant (aloe vera) to help a wound on my leg close up. I told her that I had been taking medicine to close wound for two weeks but it was taking a long time to heal. She chuckled to herself and said, "Damien, tienes que entender que los medicos no van a ensenarte los secretos naturales de la tierra porque asi no ganaran dinero". The translation was, "You have to understand that the doctors are not going to show you the natural secrets of the land because they won't make money that way."

I realized that this was the very same reason that no one in the United States had ever heard of Maca Root although, it has been sold in America for quite some time. Upon my research, I discovered that this herb could help people in more ways than just the sexual arena. Maca root is native to South America where it grows in the unique atmosphere of the Andean Mountains. It has been used as a healing herb, by the indigenous people of South America for mental, physical and sexual energies. Andean women have long used this herb to "get pregnant." Maybe the biggest reason why the herb is so revered could be the presence of almost all the essential amino acids contained within the root.

Ancient 20's 4 benefits you'll get from using Maca Root:

- Reduces Stress by Increasing Stamina – It can reduce stress by increasing mental clarity. Maca is considered as an effective adaptogenic herb, thereby can rejuvenate the tired adrenal glands. The herb can provide an energy boost to the body so as to adjust to various kinds of stress. This can help improve physical stamina, mental clarity and an improved sexual life.

- Serves as a Hormone Regulator – Rich with phytoestrogens, maca can regulate and restore the secretion of pituitary gland hormones to normal level. These phytoestrogens include such hormones as testosterone, HGH, estrogen progesterone, etc. They might help in restoring libido and improving sexual performance in both sexes.

- Natural Pain Reliever – The anti-inflammatory property of maca due to the presence of saponins, can act as a natural reliever of pain. This can help in treating arthritis pain, muscle pain, etc.

- Lower Cholesterol – It is believed that maca is a rich source of sterols. The presence of sterols might help in reducing bad cholesterol such as LDL (low-density lipoprotein).

Be advised that everything in life, if not used in some form of moderation, can be hazardous at some point. According to Chinese medicine, maca is considered as a warming herb. People having high blood pressure may want to practice caution while taking maca, as a medicine. You can buy maca in the soft capsule pill form or powder form which will be more potent. Now you have a natural herb (with no negative side-effects) to help get your energy back on track. So get moving and enjoy the things life has to offer you regardless of your age.

Law Eighteen

LOW INTENSITY CARDIO IS SUFFICIENT: "CANADA"

"A vigorous five-mile walk will do more good for an unhappy
but otherwise healthy adult than all the medicine and
psychology in the world." ~Paul Dudley White

By the time I was sixteen years old, I began to hang out with
my mother in an effort to spend more time with her. One of
my mother's favorite past times was to play the game of
bingo. As an employee of the United States Postal Service,
she had undergone many stressful days on the job. So she
relished the idea of having an extracurricular activity that
she could enjoy and win some money, at the same time.
The drawback about playing bingo in the Detroit area was
that there weren't many places where you could get a big
return for your money. In an effort to make the most of my
mother's money, we had to travel to Canada. The city of
Windsor, Ontario (Canada) was roughly a 15 minute drive
from our home. The only major issue with travel between
Detroit and Windsor was the $2.50 departing and re-
entering fees for the United States. Sometimes we got
hassled by the border patrol and delayed for an hour, but
aside from that the trip was smooth. I was also the official
"cigarette guy," for my mother when we went to Canada.
She would give me $20 which in the early 90's went a long
way and tell me to get her a cartoon of More Menthol
Cigarettes and bring her change back.

My brother and I were notorious for not returning with her change. This was a not a simple task, because while my mother was busy buying her "bingo dabbers" and "game books", I had to run and change the money from our currency to Canadian Dollars. At any rate, I was able to do it with few problems, so "Operation More Menthol" went smoothly. Windsor was an extremely clean city which was the polar opposite from Detroit. I enjoyed spending time outside, while my mother stayed inside the bingo hall. I was so sure that I had seen a major city street without a single piece of trash on it until I went to Windsor. One of my favorite past times while in Windsor, was the arcade that was directly across the street from where my mother was in the bingo parlor. The majority of the time, my mom gave me a few dollars to go to the arcade and buy something to eat. If she had won that day, then I would get maybe five dollars more so I was always wishing her good luck.

One week, I took the "bingo trip" with my mother for three days in a row. During the first day of those three days, I had seen a woman who was about 50 years of age, "fast walking" at the local school grounds that was nearby. In my mind, I figured that she was in a rush and she just needed to get to wherever she was going so I thought nothing of it. All good bingo players know that when you find a certain session that brings you luck, you tend to go to that same session each time. On the second day of the trip the same woman was "walking fast", at the same school during the same time which she had appeared the day before. Certainly there was something to this, but I could not figure it out. The thing that puzzled me the most was that I would see her and she would vanish out of my sight because she was walking away from me. Once again I continued with my daily routine and left those thoughts in Canada for that day. I generally live by the "baseball three strike rule", being that if something happens to me three times then it needs to be investigated. On the third day, I was finishing the last of some chicken nuggets from the arcade and out of the mist appeared the "mystery speed walker." But, this time she had come from another side of the street walking in her usual manner. I jogged over to see where it was that she was going, because I was really curious. I did not want to appear as though I was some kind of stalker, so I acted as if I was looking for someone at the school.

She had turned the corner and left my sight again but after 5 to 10 minutes, she came up from behind me announcing, "coming through" and I jumped out of the way. It was at that point that I realized that she must have been on some kind of exercise regimen. She finished her last lap right where I was standing and I politely asked her what all the fast walking was about. I had always known people to sprint, run, or jog but never to walk fast, so this was new to me. I said:

"Excuse me Miss but what is it that you are trying to accomplish? In a deep breathing response, she said, "Young man, I am getting my cardio in for today because my kids are at lunch. I am a teacher at this school, so I try to exercise on my lunch break for 20 minutes. Jogging would put too much pressure on my joints, so I like to walk fast to get my heart working. I used to jog 15 years ago, but chronic knee problems made me transition to speed walking. Besides, I find that speed walking is more challenging because I feel it a lot more in my hips. I have been doing this for 15 years and I have never felt better. Most people think that you have to run 4 or 5 miles every day to get in shape but I would recommend my routine to anyone who has a desire to do minimal exercise but stimulate the body."

During my time growing up, I had never known any of my elder family members to be "exercisers." They were hard workers but never were they people who owned gym memberships, or attended aerobics classes. I was happy to have found some information that I could pass on to my elders. As a sixteen year, old I believed that I was still considered a rookie when it came to health concepts and terms. I did not know what the word cardio meant, but I nodded my head as if I understood what the "speed walker" was saying when she spoke of cardio. I now know that *cardio* is short for cardiovascular, which refers to the heart. Cardiovascular exercise is exercise that raises your heart rate and keeps it elevated for a period of time. However, *aerobic exercise* can be just as potent.

Aerobic exercise improves oxygen consumption by the body. Aerobic means "with oxygen", and refers to the use of oxygen in the body's metabolic or energy-generating process. Exercises where there is no break in routine can be considered as cardiovascular. Aerobic exercise improves emotional or mental health, as well as physical health. Exercise releases *endorphins,* the so-called happiness chemicals, thus helping to improve mood and general well being.

In Law Three, I spoke about swimming, but I also realized that not everyone in this world knows how to swim or feels comfortable in water. So, I felt the need to add a chapter that would help the average person regardless of age or size. What we should understand here is that it is not necessary for you to pound on your body, or run for an hour in order to achieve a desired level of personal health and wellness. By simply walking for 20 minutes or more, for 2 to 3 times a week you can:

• Lower risk of early death

• Increase lung capacity

- Reduce the risk of heart disease

- Reduce the risk of diabetes

- Reduce blood pressure

- Have stronger bones

- Have better blood glucose control

- Have reduction in stress levels

- Enhance your immune system

- Better appetite control

- Raise metabolic rate

- Improve body fat percentage

- Lose and control weight

I am sure you have heard that you should be exercising or doing cardio everyday, but the fact remains that people are told to do things without proof or evidence of what it can do for them. The bad part is they take it at face value without searching out the reason. Get in the habit of asking questions and looking for a solution that best fits you and your life style. In truth, the harder you exercise, the more you will sweat and lose minerals. This means the higher your chances are of dying an early death. This may sound unconventional, but it is fact.

Dr. Joel Wallach, author of the heavily acclaimed book, *Dead Doctors Don't Lie,* states that the "couch potato" will outlive the athlete simply because he does not sweat out the essential nutrients and minerals that his body needs. There has not been a professional athlete to live to be 100 years old, with the exception of one Negro-League baseball player, who passed away, shortly after his 100th Birthday. This epidemic can be traced back to the lack of improper supplementation. Most individuals who exercise do not supplement properly. Exercise without proper supplementation is suicide. Let me repeat, exercise without proper supplementation is suicide!

The key point to remember is that it is good to get some exercise, for the sake of improving oxygen consumption, your mood, breaking a small sweat and strengthening your body (if so shall choose). However, over working the body will only lead to excessive loss of nutrients that the body requires. Be mindful that you MUST replenish the nutrients that your body loses during exercise. God made you a free agent to make choices for yourself, so it is only fitting that you repay the infinite intelligence with the proper care of your body. Remember that ANY form of walking is good for you. It is not necessary to walk fast. A normal walk in the park is also considered exercise. Good eating habits, coupled with mineral supplementation and proper amounts of moderate exercise go hand in hand for life longevity.

Law Nineteen

TREAT YOUR HAIR WITH RESPECT: "DUBAI"

"Hair brings one's self image into focus; it is vanity's proving
ground. Hair is terribly personal, a tangle of mysterious
prejudices." ~Shana Alexander

During the spring of 2001, I was invited to represent a
professional basketball team, from Kuwait, for a 10 team
tournament, to be held in the city of Dubai. I had no prior
knowledge of Dubai except for when I heard mention of the
PGA, the Professional Golfers Association Tour, tournament
to be held in Dubai. This city had been pegged as "the Las
Vegas of the Middle East," while boasting a $37 billion
dollar economy. Dubai is located along the southern coast
of the Persian Gulf, on the Arabian Peninsula. It is one of
seven emirates and the most populous city of the *United
Arab Emirates.* The emirate's main revenues come from
tourism, real estate, and financial services. Unlike other
Middle Eastern powerhouses, petroleum and natural gas
contributed less than 6 % of that $37 billion dollar economy
in 2005.

Dubai has a climate much like that of Kuwait, which was
very hot, so it is always best to be in doors, depending on
what time of the year you are there, until the sun goes
down. I took no issue with being inside, because the
tournament committee had arranged for all of the
participating teams to stay in a five star hotel. This hotel
had exceptional accommodations.

Each team could have 2 foreign players, so there were about

10 to 15 Americans playing in the tournament. I did not know any of the players, prior to the tournament. But, I eventually befriended some of them and we are associates to this day. The one thing that I found very interesting was that many of the Middle Eastern players looked like African Americans. This was in direct contrast to what I had seen on the news and read in the papers. I remember walking up to one of Arabic players and speaking English to him and he replied with Arabic language, as if to say that he did not understand me. One of the manager's of our team was a former player, who spoke English, so I spent a lot of time talking to him. His name was Adnon Sabey.

Adnon arranged all of the team's travel, meals, and all other team related subjects. If we needed extra money, he gave it without any questions. Mr. Sabey had a great sense of humor, because he knew what it felt like to be a player, as well. So he was not always serious with the players. One day, I decided to join Adnon for a meal in one of the hotel's many restaurants. This day we ate grilled lamb chops, which was a first for me along with an Italian side dish. Our waitress was tall, beautiful and she had smooth caramel-brown skin, but not the kind of skin of the middle easterners. Adnon noticed me staring at the young lady, so he jokingly called her over and said, "He wants to have a word with you." So now I had been put on the spot and I had to react or get laughed out of the restaurant! The waitress came to our table smiling and extended her hand, as an introduction, and she asked me, "What is your name?" I told her my name and immediately followed with, "By your looks, it doesn't appear as if you are from Dubai. Where are you from?" She said "I'm from Addis Ababa. Do you know where that is?" I countered with, "No, I am not aware of this place. Where is it located?" She went on to say that it was a city in the country of Ethiopia. Afterward, I left her to her work and told her that I would come back later to speak with her, because I was really interested in this place, Addis Ababa, Ethiopia and also interested to learn more about her. One lesson I learned that day was it doesn't matter what country you are in, guys are going to be guys. I got teased for about two days by Adnon about the young lady from Ethiopia.

Later that day, I went to eat at the same restaurant and to talk with my new friend. I found out that her name was, "*Desta*", which meant "*happiness*" in her native language. The one thing that stood out about Desta was her long, dark and curly hair. It was so wavy and smooth that it appeared as though someone had sewn her hair together from a silk material. We had a great conversation and she taught me something, which brings me to the purpose of this chapter. She taught me about "caring for my hair." I had asked her what it was that she did to have her hair look so shiny and dark and she responded with, "I have a good diet which is rich in nutrients from the earth and I do not have any bad habits, such as smoking or drinking. Many of the women that come from my country to Dubai or Europe turn to a life of corruption and pick up many of the bad habits of the western world. They love to party and chase men. In my country, we believe in God, self preservation, and strong family values. We are very cultural, when it comes to food. So, our diet is comprised of Ethiopian dishes. I realize that we are not as advanced, as those of you from the western hemisphere, but we do use all of our resources to the best of our abilities."

I was actually expecting an Ethiopian hair remedy to help my hair grow over night, but that did not happen. She encouraged me to treat my hair as though I would treat anything that I loved and respected.

Desta also mentioned some "*essential oils*" that she uses to help promote healthy beautiful hair. Her mom had used essential oils for years, as a form of hair growth promotion. Rosemary, Lavender, Cedarwood, and Thyme oil were all oils which she has seen used by Ethiopian women for hair treatments.

Over the past 7 years, I have witnessed many men and women alike, struggle with the loss of hair. In acts of desperation, they have went out and bought "miracle hair growth" products in an effort to salvage or re-grow the lost hair follicles. The problem cannot be found on the outside of your body, although you can use a few items to stimulate a healthy environment for hair growth. Hair growth encounters problems because of a breakdown within your body. Of course there are outside circumstances that play a small role in degeneration. According to expert herbalist and founder of dherbs.com, *D'Jehuty Ma'at-Ra,* there can be many types of hair problems which include:

- *Alopecia* – This is simply the falling out of patches of hair. Many people experience it, but it is more detrimental in females.

- *Split Ends* – When there are deficiencies in female ovaries, the hair will begin to split. Ovaries are a part of the hormonal system, which is also known as the *endocrine system.* If you wish to address hair problems, you must look to repair them from inside of the endocrine system. When males have split ends, it is a deficiency in the testicles.

- *Hair Fallout* – Stress and worry plays a role which means there is a connection between hair and emotions because both are connected to the endocrine system, which deals with hormones.

- *Graying Of Hair* – According to Nobel Prize nominee *Dr. Joel Wallach,* author of *Dead Doctors Don't Lie,* white,gray and silver hair is a simple copper deficiency in the diet. Graying hair is an outward sign that your health is in decline. Most individuals are warned of this health decline twenty years before the more serious effects manifest themselves.

Mr. Ma'at-Ra continues, by explaining that losing your hair can be traced to your very own daily activities which are:

- Excessive meat, dairy, grains or starch consumption – This produces excess acid in the body which the body converts into mucus. When the mucus gets into the head, it (the mucous) dries up. Because of the high mucus content in the brain, the hair follicles cannot get the necessary nutrients and oxygen, in order to grow. Thus, the hair begins to die. This is similar to a plant not receiving adequate sunshine and water.

- Harmful chemical products – Too much chemical processing of the hair greatly destroys the hair. Your hair is actually alive so when you use chemical products, you kill a part of your hair with each use. Shampoo contains many toxic ingredients in relation to the hair. They throw off the PH balance of the hair. This is the reason that the hair companies speak of their shampoos or conditioners, as PH balanced, because they know that PH balance is critical in maintaining health.

- Excessive Haircuts – There are a small percentage of men who get their hair cut once a week, but the majority of men go at least once per month. Please be advised that the *razor* that your barber uses "emits radiation." Radiation heats up the cells of the head and also kills them.

- Weaves – Some weaves are applied so tightly, that they actually pull out the hair.

- Shampoo/Conditioners – Contain toxic, harmful chemicals such as *propylene glycol* and *sodium lauryl sulfate*, are both industrial products and have no business being on the top of your head. Remember, that if you put something on your body you are putting it in your body.

You can take a breath now! The good news is that you can correct all of these situations because they only require a change of daily habit, which costs you nothing. Before I finish, I would like to touch on a subject that has puzzled many men and women around the world. I am speaking on the topic of *women with facial hair*. If you are a female and you have a bit more facial hair than you would like on your lip or on the sides of your face, science shows there is a reason for this.

D'Jehuty states, *"When women have mustaches and other facial hair, that means that she has hormonal imbalance. She is producing excess testosterone instead of progesterone. Progesterone converts into testosterone when there is a defect in the body. That defect is of a hormonal nature. Any woman who has too much hair, on the parts of her body where men should have hair, is due to too much production of the male based hormone (testosterone), which goes back to endocrine deficiency".*

If you are a female who has suffered from this condition and you want a change you now have reputable information that you can take into a *trusted health expert* to correct the problem. One of the most important things to health is finding a solution to a problem.

These 6 tips can help you strengthen your endocrine system to reverse any hair loss that you may experience:

- Choose your food intelligently. Eat as organically as possible and minimize animal fat consumption. Because endocrine disruptors and heavy metals magnify in the food chain, the higher your protein source, the greater the potential toxic load.

- If you can't buy all organic food, try to pick and choose.

- Take a wide-spectrum daily multivitamin with essential fatty acids – to ensure rich nutrition and support your body's optimal functioning.

- Support your body's natural ability to detox, by exercising and sweating on a regular basis. Try a gentle detox program a few times a year. Also, use a sauna or a steam bath.

- Investigate the chemicals in your cosmetics, bug spray, lotions and toiletries.

- Supplement with minerals! The root of ALL hair problems stem from the lack of the proper nutrients within the body.

Everyone has been taught that hair loss is hereditary, which may have a degree of truth to it. The human mind is an incredible instrument that is capable of overcoming any obstacle. With the correct amount of faith and information, all things are possible. If you are a male, who suffers from male pattern baldness, you may also want to look into the trace mineral, known as tin. Joel Wallach, of the *Dead Doctors Don't Lie* fame, claims that significant hair re-growth can be stimulated following tin supplementation in a multi-mineral vitamin tablet or a complete mineral vitamin product. The stimulation of hair growth by tin at high dilutions is not an unfounded idea. The basis for this claim was originally reported by Dr. Schwarz who observed hair loss resembling male-pattern baldness in tin deficient rats. These findings were subsequently confirmed in a 1990 study by Yokoi of Kyoto University.

Be sure to focus on those nutrients that feed the *GONADS* (ovaries and testicles) because the base of all hair problems can be traced back to endocrine system deficiencies.

Law Twenty

MINERALS AND FLEXIBILTY, THE LONGEVITY SECRET: "SPAIN"

"God sleeps in the minerals, awakens in plants, walks in animals, and thinks in man." ~Arthur Young

If I am not mistaken, there is a saying that says, "all that glitters ain't gold." I am a living witness that the statement rings true. I have had a great time traveling the world and playing professional basketball, but the reality is that job security was at times, extremely uncertain. The dilemma with being a professional basketball player in Europe, is that you will more than likely change locations every two years or so. In my case I have never played two consecutive seasons in one country (with the exception of the Dominican Republic). Often times you pass the time waiting for a phone call from your agent about from where your next potential contract could come. Those are some of the more difficult times, because your bills are constantly coming in but your pay checks are not! What's worse is that if you have an injury, your contract is not fully guaranteed and sometimes you could be sent home to pay for your own doctor bill, especially if your contract is not negotiated correctly.

It is from those times that I came to learn one of the most valuable lessons with regard to my health and my career. It was the lesson of supplementing with minerals every day to avoid any physical breakdowns within the body. Most European leagues start up in October. So, when you are sitting at home in November you know that you have missed the "first wave jobs". Your only chance to get signed to a good contract is for someone to get injured (which I would never want). Or another chance to get signed is for a team to be dissatisfied with a player's performance and send him home (which happens very often). Some teams always griped about paying an airline ticket just to bring a player in for a tryout so the next logical thing would be to "get to Europe" in an effort to lower the team's expenses and greater your chance of a tryout.

A genius idea was if a player knew someone who was living in Europe, the player could fly himself over to live with them and put himself in close proximity of the European teams. This is exactly what I did. I had just so happened to be recovering from an injury so I needed to put myself in a favorable situation to get a job. I was fortunate, because I had two great friends of mine living in Valencia, Spain. They invited me to come and stay with them and I was pleased and obliged. They were a married couple whom had become like my very own family. Actually, the wife, (Chelle), had just finished a season in the Women's National Basketball Association (WNBA) and was just starting another season in Spain. Her husband (Sheldon) entertained contract offers, as well, but had not yet signed to a team. He welcomed the opportunity to work out with me, while we both awaited the tryouts.

Chelle was a great player, whom I had not known much about prior to us meeting many years ago. In fact I had no knowledge of women making money playing professionally overseas. Was I wrong! She currently plays in the WNBA, where she has won 2 WNBA championships. During her career, she has garnered; 2 Olympic gold medals, a bronze medal from the FIBA World Championships, the 1997 State Farm Wade Trophy winner (an award presented annually to the best women's college basketball player in NCAA division 1), the 1997 SEC Player of the Year, 1st team All-SEC, 1st team All-Euroleague, Euroleague champion (twice) and many more accomplishments. As one may notice, she is a very accomplished individual. So, when she lends advice, it is always best to listen. When I arrived in Valencia, Chelle and Sheldon sat me down on the couch after dinner to have a talk with me. They are people who have always had my best interest, because of this I listened eagerly as always. Chelle said to me in a concerned voice:

"Damien, you have to do something about these injuries that you are getting. Every time we look up, you are injured. You are physically in great shape, on the outside, but there is obviously a breakdown about which you are unaware. How could a guy be as ripped up as you are with all those muscles, stay injured? You are not taking care of your body, or eating right. Maybe you eat some healthy things, but you must remember that you are a Lamborghini but you are refueling your body, as if you were a Pinto. Are you taking minerals? Do you stretch before and after every practice, or when you are at home doing nothing? You, of all people, should know that your body will only give out what you put in it."

I could do nothing but sit there and listen. I had watched those friends take liquid minerals and essential fatty acid capsules every morning and night but I had not taken heed to what they were doing. Many times, when we were watching NBA games, via satellite, Chelle would sit in the middle of the floor and stretch, while talking with me and her spouse. There was no wonder why she had been so successful. She gives the glory and honor to God, but she followed that by saying "I am always conscious of taking minerals and stretching after practices. I have to replenish my body with all of the nutrients that I lose through sweating. If I don't do one of these two things, I tend to feel sluggish. As I get older, I definitely do not want to pull a muscle warming up for a game, so I take these two subjects very serious."

Sheldon reminded me that, it was I who had gotten them to be very conscious of taking minerals and focused on nutrition. At some point, I had fallen off of the wagon. Three years before my trip to Spain, Sheldon called me and informed me that Chelle was having constant pain in her knees. A year prior to his call, I had heard a CD titled *Dead Athletes Don't Lie* by a doctor known as "The Mineral Doctor". His name was Dr. Joel Wallach BS, DVM, ND. Wallach's approach was simple. He felt that IF exercising was the way to go, then how could so many athletes, in top physical condition, die from playing sports? The answers which linked athlete related deaths and injuries could be traced back to a LACK OF MINERALS and vitamins.

Dr. Wallach also felt that instead of giving patients drugs and putting a bandage over the problem, he decided to fix the problem and solve it, so the problem would never come back. He did this with mineral supplementation. Most doctors would try to operate on your "bad knee cartilage", where as Doctor Wallach would give you the nutritional supplements to repair the cartilage and give the body an environment to promote cartilage regrowth. What makes Wallach's approach unique is that he is a physician, veterinarian, and has a degree in agriculture with a minor in field crops & soils, so he covers all aspects of the medical spectrum.

Dr. Wallach is also famous in the basketball world for resurrecting the career of NBA (National Basketball Association) star Theo Ratliff, after several bouts with career ending knee and bone issues. Theo was set to retire at the ripe old age of 27. That was until he met Dr. Wallach.

Needless to say, Theo has played more than 10 years and earned more than 75 million dollars in salary from the NBA, since his "career ending knee injuries." I figured, if Wallach could help Theo, then he could certainly help Chelle! After connecting with Dr. Wallach, her career has blossomed to another level. In fact, she has had her best individual statistical years, since getting on the "Wallach Mineral Program." She also has not experienced any further injuries. This is extremely significant considering that most athletes begin to decline once they reach their thirties. Chelle has gotten better after her thirties. After our talk on the couch, I made it a point to get on *Wallach's Mineral Program* and I have been very pleased with the results. These very same minerals are what brought me back from the injury that doctors said had ended my career.

According to Wikipedia.com the definition of a *Multivitamin is a preparation intended to supplement a human diet with vitamins, dietary minerals and other nutritional elements. Such preparations are available in the form of tablets, capsules, pastilles, powders, liquids and inject able formulations, which are only available and administered under medical supervision, multivitamins are recognized by the Codex Alimentarius Commission (the United Nations highest authority on food standards) as a category of food. Multivitamin supplements are commonly provided in combination with minerals.*

There was a research done that showed:

"People who take a multivitamin every day have *telomere lengths* that are five percent longer than those who get their vitamins and nutrients only through diet." Telomere length is an important marker for cellular aging. A *telomere* is a portion of DNA that protects the chromosomes from damage and destruction. As cells become older, the telomeres shorten in length. This is considered to be an accurate sign of a cell that's past its prime. Telomere length is thought to be a marker for cellular aging".

Although these results are interesting, it doesn't necessarily indicate that the longer telomeres seen in multivitamin users were actually caused by taking vitamins. Generally, people who take multivitamins on a regular basis eat a healthier diet and have an overall healthier lifestyle, which could also be why their cells age more slowly.

Eating a healthy diet from the four main food groups is not enough to give you longevity. You must supplement with real minerals/nutrients, in order to get all that the body requires. It is essential that one grasps this concept. The soil that is currently being used to grow our foods is no longer the same soil in which our ancestors once grew crops. The soil is now tainted with fertilizers and toxic growth chemicals and depleted of minerals therefore, leaving the vegetation nutrient deficient.

Aside from taking minerals, Chelle attributes stretching as her secret weapon to success. Stretching will surely enhance your overall well being because it allows your body to absorb more contact. Your body is a very complex machine that is connected from head to toe. If one thing is out of alignment and stiff, then it is certain to cause pain and stiffness in other areas of your body, because the body will have to over compensate for the lack of production of that particularly part.

Take a glance at what stretching can do for the body:

• Reduce muscle tension

• Increase range of motion in your joints

• Enhance muscular coordination

• Increase circulation of the blood to various parts of the body

- Increase energy levels

- Relaxation and stress relief

- Pain relief

Everyone can learn to stretch, regardless of age or flexibility. Stretching should be a part of your daily routine, whether you exercise or not. There are simple stretches you can do, while watching TV, on the computer, or getting ready for bed. In their book, *Faster Flexibility,* authors *Mary Shells and Gregory Finn* give four, of many heavy hitting benefits of stretching.

According to *Faster Flexibility*, stretching can:

- *Correct Muscular Imbalances* – Correct posture is the number one most critical factor to a healthy structure. Muscular imbalances cause muscle pairs to work against each other instead of with each other. Lower back problems, knee injuries, and chronic shoulder ailments all begin rehabilitation by restoring muscular balance to the entire body, through a dedicated stretching program.

- *Prevent Injury* – We all know that accidents occur most unexpectedly and without warning. A twisted ankle, or a hyper-extended wrist are both injuries that can be prevented by increasing flexibility around the joints. Sprains, twist and pulls do not occur unless the muscle or connective tissue is brought past its flexibility extreme. It becomes obvious that increased range of motion can decrease chance of injury to the joints and surrounding tissues.

- *Increase Physical Awareness* – Regular stretching will help to reduce muscle tension. This will aid the connection between the muscular skeletal system and the nervous system, through the reduction of the inefficient firing of neurons. Overtime, the practice of concentration while stretching strengthens the mental connection between the nervous system and muscular skeletal system, eventually reaching a level unprecedented.

- *Increased Speed and Agility* – Working towards developing levels of flexibility will result in decreased muscle tension throughout the body. Muscles work in pairs. The triceps must relax, in order for the biceps to contract. How rapidly the biceps can contract, is somewhat dependent on how rapidly the triceps can relax. This is how a reduced muscle tension can help to increase the overall contraction speed of a muscle group.

It has been a pleasure to take you along with me through 20 countries of memories and stories of health. Let this book be a blessing to you and may it enhance your life and the life of your loved ones. Blessings! Again, my goal through this book is to explore natural health and make it a way of life.

ABOUT THE AUTHOR

Damien Douglas McSwine is a health researcher, as well as professional athlete. After receiving his BA in Criminal Justice from Loyola University, Chicago in 2001, Damien decided to postpone a trip to the Kent School of Law, to pursue a career in professional basketball. After a foot injury threatened to end his career, McSwine went on to do the unthinkable and became the first professional athlete ever documented, to play a sport with a titanium total toe joint replacement. Damien attributes a big part of his recovery to prayer, nutrient supplementation and the application of many of the health laws he learned while traveling abroad. It was during a two year comeback that he made the decision to put these laws into book form and share them with others.

He feels very privileged to have had a golden opportunity to capture valuable information and convey a message to those in need. Through extensive research and studies, the author has seen the power of extraordinarily simple steps, proper nutrition and nutrient supplementation as they relate to health. During the 7 years he studied under his personal mentor, *Nobel Prize Nominee*, Dr. Joel Wallach, Damien learned that there are over 800 diseases and ailments that can be prevented through proper nutrition and nutrient supplementation.

McSwine credits leading health experts like Dr. Joel Wallach, Gary Null, Dick Gregory, Djehuty Ma'at-ra, Joel Fuhrman MD and Jay "The Juice Man" Kordich as the individuals who had the biggest impact on him as a health researcher.

BIBLIOGRAPHY

BOOKS

- Agin, Brent and Shereen Jegtvig. *Superfoods For Dummies* (Wiley, John & Sons, Inc., USA: 2009).

- Appleton, Nancy. *Lick The Sugar Habit* (Penguin Group, USA: 1988).

- Cohen, Robert. *Milk The Deadly Poison* (Argus Publishing, Inc., Eaglewood Cliffs, NJ: 1997).

- Ingram, Cass. *The Cure Is in the Cupboard* (Knowledge House Publishers, USA: 1996).

- Kordich, Jay. *The Juiceman's Power Of Juicing* (Warner Books Inc., New York, NY: 1993).

- Mak, Stephen. *Eating Fruits. no. 1* (Article) www.awayoflife.net 2010

- Rombauer, Irma S. and Marion Rombauer Becker. *Joy of Cooking* (Simon and Schuster, New York: 1997).

- Wallach, J.D. and Ma Lan, M.D., *Hell's Kitchen* (Wellness Publications, LLC. Bonita, CA: 2002)

- Shells, Mary and Gregory Finn. *Faster Flexibility* (BOOKSHOCK Publications, Toronto, ON: 2002).

- Sherman, Henry C.. *Chemistry Of Food And Nutrition* (The MacMillan Co., New York, NY: 1912).

- Wattles, Wallace. *The Science Of Being Well* (Elizabeth Towne Co., Massachusetts: 1910).

- Wallach, J.D. and Ma Lan, M.D., *Dead Doctors Don't Lie* (Legacy Communications Group, Inc., Franklin, TN: 1999).

- Widner, E.A.. *Pork, Man and Disease: Good Health, Volume 69, no.1* (Article).

- Wallach, J.D., Ma Lan, M.D. and Daniels, Jennifer, M.D.. *Black Gene Lies: Slave Quarter Cures* (Wellness Publications, LLC. Bonita, CA: 2006).

WEBSITES

<u>Law One</u>

- "It is noteworthy to know that the human body............"

  http://epa.gov/WaterSense/water/benefits.htm

<u>Law Two</u>

- "Sleep is a time to help your body repair itself............."

  http://www.associatedcontent.com/article/178456/the_hea lth_benefits_of_sleep.html?cat =25 (AC Associated Content)

- "It seems as though you are shifting memory to more efficient............"

  http://webmd.com/sleep-disorders/news/200506291how- sleep-helps-memory-learning

- "Those who sleep less than 5 hours.........."

  http://www.sciencedaily.com/releases/2006/05/06052908 2903.htm

<u>Law Three</u>

- "Swimming improves the body's oxygen use and ...."

http://www.24hrfitness.co.uk/fitness/the-benefits-of-swimming.html

(24 Hr Fitness.co.uk)

Law Four

- "Encourage eating whole grain breads because..............."

http://www.wholegrainscouncil.org/

Law Five

- "Moreover, tap water has to meet a certain health code as far as the filtration process........."

www.communitywater.com (Community Water Company of Green Valley)

- "Bottled water and tap water are regulated by two different agencies ...."

http://www.hhs.gov/asl/testify/2009/07/t20090708a.html

Law Eight

- "Studies undertaken on healthy subjects and patients with gastro ...."

www.internationaloliveoil.org/ (International Olive Oil Council)

Law Nine

- "1. Walnuts – Contain an antioxidant called *ellagic acid* that supports the immune system ...."

www.teachingpriest.org

Law Ten

- "Honey is also comprised of minerals like magnesium, potassium, calcium, sodium, chlorine, sulfur ...."

http://www.beesonline.oo.nz/ (Bees-Online), http://thomashoney.com/honey_bees.html, www.islamic-world.net/

Law Twelve

- "Wild oregano is veritable, a natural mineral treasure-house ...."

http://www.homeremediesweb.com/oil_of_oregano_health_benefits.php

Law Thirteen

- "a problem with bladder storage function that causes a sudden urge to urinate."

http://www.mayoclinic.com/health/overactive-bladder/DS00827

Law Fourteen

- "Red meat may increase the likelihood of cancer.....". *http://news.bbc.co.uk/hi/health/4088824.stm (BBC NEWS ARTICLE)*

- "Chicken is the world's primary source of animal protein.....".

www.whfoods.org (World's Healthiest Foods)

- "Eating fish can provide an excellent source of providing Omega-3 fatty acids..."

www.doh.wa.gov/ehp/oehas/fish/fishbenefits.htm (Washington State Department of Health)

Law Fifteen

- "Sweet Potatoes are relatively low in calories and have no fat......".

  www.vegetarian-nutrition.info/updates/onions.php

Law Sixteen

- "New data shows that the average U.S. adults consumes.........".

  www.webmd.com (WebMD)

- "Sixty people with type 2 diabetes took 1,3, or 6 grams of cinnamon........".

  http://hubpages.com/hub/Health_Benefits_of_Grapefruit

Law Seventeen

- "It has been used as a healing herb by the indigenous people of South America........".

  http://herbs.ygoy.com/2009/02/18/health-benefits-of-maca-root/

Law Eighteen

- "Cardiovascular exercise is exercise that raises your heart rate and keeps it elevated......".

  http://pilates.about.com/od/pilatesforeverybody/alcardio.htm

Law Nineteen

- "Stress and worry plays a role which means there is a connection between........".

www.dherbs.com (DHERBS), *http://en.wikipedia.org/wiki* (Wikipedia)

- "Significant hair re-growth can be stimulated following tin........."

www.thewallachfiles.com

Law Twenty

- "A multivitamin is a preparation intended to supplement a human diet with vitamins.......".

http://en.wikipedia.org/wiki/Multivitamin

- "People who take a multivitamin everyday have *telomere lengths* that are five.......".

http://vitamins-minerals.suite101.com/article.cfm/should_you_take_a_multivitamin